A

MW01006167

HAJJ

Reflections on its Rituals

Translated by
Laleh Bakhtiar

Introduction by
Sayyid Gulzar Haider

ABJAD

Albuquerque, N.M. 87196

Published by:

ABJAD
P. O. Box 40052
Albuquerque, NM 87196

Library of Congress Cataloging-in Publication Data
Ali Shariati, b. 1934
    [Tahlili az manasik-i-hajj. English]
    Hajj: Reflections on its Rituals/ Ali Shariati: translated by
Laleh Bakhtiar.
        p. cm. 22
        Translation of: Tahlili az manasik-i-hajj.
        Includes bibliographical references (p.)
        ISBN 1-871031-03-6
        1. Muslim pilgrims and pilgrimages—Arabia—Mecca. 2.
    Muslim rituals. I. Laleh Bakhtiar. II. Title.
    English

BP 187.3   .S4986   1992

Distributed by:

Kazi Publications, Inc.
3023-27 W. Belmont Ave.
Chicago, IL 60618

CONTENTS

DEDICATION

To the barefooted believer who,
trapped in the toils of existence,
remains thirsty for Zamzam—
To the awakened soul who,
having seen the vision of an *ummah*
rising from the plain of Arafah,
remains locked out of the Haram—
To the son of Abraham who,
having declared the liberation from idols
of the East and the West,
is forced to silent obedience
before the gatekeepers of the Ka'bah—
To the daughter of Hagar who
cannot find her footprints—
To the sister of Khadijah who
searches her threshold in vain—
To the forgotten brother of Bilal who
longs for his voice—
To the cast-down gaze that
seeks the path of the Prophets—
And to the expectant hands that
rise in supplication—
This book is presented
with hope.

INTRODUCTION

Muslims of our epoch are in an abject state of loss. Where there should have been life-giving certainty of belief in the Divine Creator and His Purpose, there are gnawing doubts and ambivalence.

Apologetic about their religion, they excuse themselves in a thousand and one ways. They feel unarmed against the onslaught of theological pluralism, secular humanism, hedonistic materialism, scientific determinism and numerous expressions of man-in-defiance of God. Most seek refuge in the romantically perfect versions of a laundered history. And some withdraw into universalist neo-mysticism that thrives in grayness achieved in the name of simultaneous tolerance of totally opposing ideologies.

The Holy Quran has been reduced to a book of *barakah* (grace), calligraphed and printed in multi-colors, wrapped in silk, and lyrically recited, without understanding, at ceremonies of initiation, rejoicing and mourning. The Prophet Muhammad (ص) is treated with superficial reverence that excuses Muslims from the challenge of following his steadfast and unwavering example. His *sunnah* is reduced to a literal time and place-bound biography that is selectively invoked to rationalize a wide range of behavior. His life has been atomized into minutiae of disjoined anecdotes and parables. Both the Revelation as Eternal Quran and the Prophet as the Perfect Man, indeed, the Living Quran, are tyrannized and, through selective and self-serving interpretations of the 'court ulama', have been defaced beyond recognition.

Muslims, quick to quote their Prophet about acquisition of knowledge, remain ignorant, even illiterate. From banal to brilliant, they speak of *ummah*, its oneness, its indivisibility and its common destiny and yet they are split among forty-six nation states who viciously guard their 'sovereignty' with total disregard for the interests of the *ummah*. They bow before the false gods of nation, language and culture and carry on their intrigues and vendettas reminiscent of the Age of Ignorance (*jahiliyyah*).

Totally immersed in the secular developmental paradigm, completely convinced that 'contemporary reality' demands allegiance to either one or the other of the big powers, the governments of the Muslim world treat their Islam as an outdated set of rituals to which the masses are historically addicted. Deep down they know that Islam must be contained in the boundaries of the beautiful mosques and must not be allowed to rise from the prayer rug. Their 'scholars' and 'religious thinkers' are kept occupied in internally neutralized symposia and hastily formed think tanks. The governors, policy makers and even teachers are professional mercenaries who are quick to plead ignorance and even disgust with the realm of Islam. The study of Islam has been reduced to institutes of 'Islamic Studies' that are busy serving either the non-Muslim orientalists who pose as objective scholars or are employed by the governments who are in need of speech-writers, good at hiding any policy or action with 'Islamic wrappings'.

Islamic scholarship, worthy of its title, has been at best crippled and made anemic. With very few exceptions, the naive are being led by the semi-ignorant, charlatans are posing as Islamic leaders, yesterday's loyal servants of the enemy have changed their garb, memorized some verses and, *ad nauseam*, talk of an Islamic renaissance. Their slogans are hollow, their hearts are weak and their souls have been sold to many gods. The 'Muslim nation' while it speaks of *'pan-ummatic'* goals is entangled in a myriad of internal contradictions. It has no identity, no selfhood, no oneness. It has wrapped the Quran in silk and has shelved it. It has imprisoned the Prophet to remote memory and forgotten its covenant with God. With its head comfortable in the lap of a God-less enchantress, in a state of materialistic trance, it daydreams of the Prophet's Madinah, long gone, or a future 'Islamopolis' still unchartered. It is stranded in a sea of hypocrisy in the darkness of self-deception.

O the Courage that questions Islam about Muslims and the
*   Muslims about Islam*
O the Wisdom that shatters the facades of ignorance, and

> *touches the injured spirits*
> *O the Light that awakens the hopes once again and*
> *brightens the tomorrow of this eclipsed today.*

Ali Shariati personifies the lament of our epoch and the light of the grottos of our existence. Aglow with the faith and courage of an Abu Dharr, he appears in our darkness and awakens us from our comforted slumber. His inflamed rhetorics light a million torches. He touches the youthful hearts of his time until they feel the resonant unity of purpose. Leaving a trail of piercing questions, exhortations, analyses, supplications, metaphors and images, he crosses the threshold of time. And now he lives with a presence stronger than life. His courage, his wisdom and his light will contribute to the energy of the Islamic movement in far places and in distant times. Tomorrow's history will judge, with gratitude and reverence, this *mujahid* of today.

Ali Shariati is a teacher who journeys hard in search of knowledge and a believer for whom every new realization is only to enhance his certainty in the monotheistic Truth. He is a Muslim in the finest sense of the word. A lover of the Beloveds of God and their pious tradition, he has suffered the sufferings of exile and the tortures of prisons to find and uphold the Truth and speak for the rights of the dispossessed. His words are not hollow literature, nor his thoughts some soap-box polemics. His theories are not speculative nor his ideas mere musings of an arm-chair angry-man living in remote comfort.

In the isolation of the prison cell, through the hardships of being hunted, in the agony of exile, in the silence of his prayers and *Hajj*, not once but three times, in his perpetual revolution against the *taghut* of this world, at home, abroad and everywhere, Shariati reflects upon history, sculpts his ideas and formulates his unique expression of the monotheistic worldview.

He studies the Quran and derives from it a theory of history as well as the lessons for the responsible intellectual. He imagines traveling a whole month with the Beloved Prophet Muhammad and attains a mystic's glimpse of his personality and socio-political wisdom. He rediscovers Abu Dharr Ghifari and Salman Farsi and sets standards of devotion to the Prophet and dedication to the Way of Islam. He goes back to the trials and tribulations of early Islam, again and again, and wonders about the parallels of those times with ours. He falls in love with the wisdom, the truth and the perseverance of Ali ibn Abi Talib. He recognizes, in his anguish, the agony and aloneness of this great *mu'min* and Companion of the Prophet. He imagines to be with Husayn ibn Ali and in his caravan's dust he sees the most precious visions of an eternal Islamic movement against tyranny and injustice. In the lives of Fatimah and Zaynab, Shariati sees the archetypal Muslim women, related to one another through Husayn: one, the architect of his being and his character, the other, the bearer of his martyrdom's message across land and time.

Ali Shariati loves the Prophet, his *ahl al-bayt* and pious Companions. He sees them as visages of God's intention for man. Though he grows up in the Shi'ite milieu, he takes issue with the tightly bound, overly ritualized, socio-politically castrated 'dark Shi'ism', as he calls it. With his brilliant analysis of the early history of Islam, in the overall framework of monotheism and the Prophet's revolution, he presents a radically different view of the martyrdom of Husayn ibn Ali. In the perseverance of Ali and Abu Dharr, in the battleground of Siffin, in the happenings of Karbala and in the confrontations in the court of Damascus, he sees the process of safeguarding Islam against the internal tendencies of selfish innovation and reversion to tribal *jahiliyyah*.

Shariati always transcends the particulars of a historic event and draws the principles that are as eternal as Islam. In this, he does enjoy the methodological support of the Holy Quran itself. In every age, he says, we must behave as if the movement of monotheism (*tawhid*) is alive but under threat. As the revolution of Islam keeps unfolding, the friends of God still stand steadfast, though usually alone. There is still a call for ultimate affirmation of the Truth through martyrdom as oppressed mankind waits for the voice and the hand that will unmask the thousand faces of tyranny.

Shariati's *Hajj* is a journey, a directed movement, nay, a transcendent elevation of his very being. He resolves on it repeatedly and returns to invite us to be Abraham-like, to cast away our 'me-ness', to make a *bay'at* (covenant) with the 'Right Hand of God', to become one *ummah* and discard multitheism forever, to seek the direction and understand the movement from knowledge to consciousness to love, to will the sacrifice of 'our Ishmael' in order that we acquire the courage to snatch away the sword from the hand of the *taghut* and never to cease the battle with the 'triple-headed *Iblis* of **Despotism, Exploitation** and **Deception**'.

Perhaps Shariati's most outstanding characteristic, that which distinguishes him and puts him in the ranks of Muhammad Iqbal Lahori[1] and Shahid Ustad Murtaza Mutahhari[2] is that his faith provides him the courage to study all ideologies without fear or malice. And this precisely is the secret of his being able to, so clearly, arrive at and succinctly express the essence of Islam. He does not have to resort to the double-talk of the apologists or the closed-minded, sword-swinging of those who can only glorify Islam by damning all else. Shariati compares religions with other religions and comes to the conclusion that for One Allah there can only be One Direction, only One Universal Purpose. He studies Iqbal and Jamal al-Din Afghani and others before him who have concerned themselves with the plight of the Muslim. He studies Western and Eastern philosophies. He pours over histories of nations. He wonders about cultures, politics, freedoms, rights, progress and decline. He never loses either courage or curiosity for understanding the nature of the human being, his destiny, his temptations and his spiritual limits. From these journeys of the mind and heart, aided by his study of the Quran and the contemplation on the nature of Prophethood, Divine Guidance and its continuation, he comes back with the eternal confrontation between Cain and Abel, Pharaoh and Moses, Nimrod and Abraham, the idolators of Makkah, the hypocrites of Madinah and the Blessed Prophet Muhammad (ص). He discovers then that the addressees of the Divine Revelation are *al-nas*, the people of the earth. He becomes suspicious of the intellections of the elite. He identifies the four prisons of mankind, bemoans alienated man, translates the *Wretched of the Earth*, criticizes existentialism and exposes Marxism and other Western fallacies.

But he always returns to his Ka'bah, the center of the
constellation of his thoughts: Abrahamic monotheism.
And again and again he returns to the legacy of the
revolution of Muhammad (ﷺ) and its timeless challenge to multitheism in its countless manifestations.

Of his ideas, he gives generously through his lectures in the universities at Mashhad and Tehran. When
they take him away from his students, he writes for
them. When they take the classroom away from him, he
goes to Husayniyah Irshad[3] and his students flock
around him. When they take away the pen, he records
his voice. And when he can no longer perform any
aspect of his mission, he, too, Prophet-like, migrates.
For Ali Shariati, knowing, being, becoming and struggling for justice are all together and inseparable. He
neither submits nor does he beg favors except from the
One God. Unshakable in his belief, disciplined in thought,
patient in his suffering, overflowing with love for the
Quran and its humanly manifest perfections like
Abraham, Hagar, Ishmael, Muhammad (ﷺ), his Household and his Companions like Abu Dharr, Ali Shariati
comes very close to the Iqbalian ideal of an Islamic
selfhood. Shariati, for his own time, becomes the
Zindeh-Rud (Living Stream) of Iqbal's *Javid-Nameh* and
Jalal al-Din Rumi would introduce him in the following
way:

A grain of sand is he
That soars in heavens and contains a world
Of longing in his heart. Naught will he see
Except his inner self, and unpledged is his soul
Unburdened, free; the wide-expanse of life

He swiftly doth traverse, its vastness all.
In fancy I do call him 'Living Stream'.[4]

Shariati became the embodiment of Iqbal's exhortation in *Israr-i-khudi*:

Be a lover constant in devotion to thy Beloved,
That thou mayst cast thy noose and capture God.
Sojourn for a while on the Hira of the heart,
Abandon self and flee to God.
Strengthened by God, return to thy self
And break the heads of the Lat and Uzza of sensuality.
By the might of Love ,evoke an army,
Reveal thyself on the Faran of Love,
That the Lord of the Ka'bah may show thee favor
And interpret to thee the test, 'Lo, I will appoint a
Vicegerent on the earth'.[5]

History will judge Shariati's *Hajj* as one of the most important documents of Islamic renaissance. While a great deal of his work has come to us as transcriptions of his lectures, *Hajj*, however, is a book that he is blessed with some time to work on. It is, along with *Martyrdom* and *Once Again Abu Dharr*, among the most representative of his thought and his philosophy.

It is difficult, if not outright impossible, to subject Shariati's writings to any kind of structural analysis. He obviously does not write for the 'reviewers of scholarly journals and academic publishing houses'. His work is a unique synthesis of the lessons of an inspiring teacher, exhortations of a revolutionary, devotions of an absorbed-believer and theories of a social philosopher who wants to be understood by *al-nas*, the people of this earth. He cannot be paraphrased without a serious loss of the power of his message. With full cognizance of the danger, I outline below what I consider to be the visages of *Hajj*, the book:

1. It presents, on the stage of history, Abraham and Ishmael to construct a model of a *mu'min*: a believing human being; an *imam*: a leader; and a *mujahid*: a soldier of the monotheistic movement. All other characters and settings appear only to make us recognize the deeper significance of the Abrahamic maker. From the defiant confrontation with the self-proclaimed god, Nimrod, to the exiles, wanderings, separations, supplications and battles with Iblis, we are led to participate in the most awe-inspiring test of belief in the One and Only God Who has no partners, that is, the sacrifice of Ishmael. Abraham becomes the manifest legacy of monotheistic man's relationship with his God. And what is the reward of all this? The Station of the Friend of God, the commission to become figuratively and literally the architect of the 'House of God' on this earth, the leadership of the nations of believers, a progeny of Prophets and Messengers and, perhaps, most important of all, eternity in the hearts of mankind through the *hajj*— when a human being believes like Abraham (ε), lives and leads like Muhammad (ص), is subservient and steadfast like Ali (ε), and is ever-prepared to offer his very being like Ishmael (ε) and Husayn (ε).

Through *Hajj*, Shariati comments on history's socio-political constants. Mankind has always had its Cain, the owner, the landlord, the usurper, the exploiter and the murderer. He rides on the back of Abel, the dispossessed, the peasant, the exploited, the robbed and the massacred. The deceitful and cunning 'fox', the coercive and despotic 'wolf' and the greedy and exploitative 'rat' rule over the submissive and humiliated 'lamb', the people. Man becomes the plaything of Iblis who appears in all times and in numerous garb from fearsome Pharaonic arrogance to seductively liberal, God-less humanism.

The human being, Shariati repeatedly emphasizes, is to become free only through the destruction of all idols, cleaning his 'house' from all that distracts him from his Creator, sacrificing all bonds that tie him down to his false hopes and only then, through the monotheistic transformation of his being, acquiring the courage to dislodge the tyranny and emerge from the dark night of falsehood. Only then does the lamb stand fearlessly before the wolf.

"Whoever submits his whole self to God
And is a doer of good
Will get his reward with his Lord (that is)
There shall be no fear, nor shall there be grief. "(2:112)

3. *Hajj* is a blueprint for the Islamic movement and monotheistic revolution. To Shariati, God is the Eternal Constancy and man, the eternal movement. The notions of *resolve, direction, movement* and then a higher resolve, more focused direction and a more forceful movement appear as a convergent spiral all through his writings. Muslims, these pilgrims, these isolated, fortified, discriminating and discriminated crowd of individualities resolve to cast off their masks, put on the *ihram* and

become the 'white sown fields of monotheism'. The experience transforms the individuals into the *ummah*, the cells into the body. The negation of all is essential to accepting the One and then becoming one. There is a definite direction but not a destination. There are many stations of realizations and many pauses of reflection but no end of the journey.

In this sense, Hajj is not a pilgrimage to a shrine because the Ka'bah is anti-relativistic. One resolves to journey to the Ka'bah only to discover the direction of life's journey, to establish the meaning of one's existence and to reflect upon the many visages of the enemy. *Hajj* is the beginning of a migration, from narcissistic self-adoration to the search for the Face of the Beloved, from meekness to fearlessness, from ambivalence to resolve, from multitheism to monotheism. *Hajj* is the journey of the isolated individuality in the direction of a cohesive *ummah*.

The pilgrimage enlightens the minds of the Faithful:
It teaches separation from one's home and destroys attach-
      ment to one's native land;
It is an act of devotion in which all feel themselves to be one,
It binds together the leaves of the book of religion.

"*Hajj* is movement from self, towards God, in the company of the people." *Hajj* is movement, movement is Islam, Islam is the Way and its orientation is monotheism; the Quran is the light, the Prophets are the guides and Imams, the leaders—in all times and everywhere. God is the only Constancy and creation is a perpetual movement.

God's creation is not chaos but order and direction, not turbidity but ever-unfolding freshness. It is here that Shariati comes closest to Iqbal's dynamic conception of the universe, Ibn Maskawaih's view of life as an evolutionary movement and al-Bairuni's concept of nature as a process of becoming. Listen to Iqbal:

Islam demands loyalty to God, not to thrones. And since God is the ultimate spiritual basis of all life, loyalty to God virtually amounts to a man's loyalty to his own ideal nature. The ultimate spiritual basis of all life, as conceived by Islam, is eternal and reveals itself in variety and change. A society based on such a conception of Reality must reconcile, in its life, the categories of permanence and change. It must possess eternal principles to regulate its collective life, for the eternal gives us a foothold in the world of perpetual change."[6]

In *Ramuz-i-bikhodi*, Iqbal devotes a complete section of his *mathnawi* to significances of the Sacred House (*bayt al-haram*) and the Ka'bah as the essential center of Muslim collective identity and in his inimitable style exhorts the sick nation to find its health and vitality by resolving for the hajj.

4. The most brilliant and courageous aspect of hajj is the way it extracts—from every act and sequence, every day and duration, every path and place, every personage and event and even the flowing river of pilgrims— a symbol of universal significance. It is here that Shariati has broken away from the tradition of dry, lifeless and overly scholastic philosophers and protagonists of Islam. He puts forward a new language and a fresh methodology of looking at what everybody apologeti-

cally calls the 'rituals of pilgrimage'.

He also departs from the tradition of romantic and devotional literature that describes the peak emotions of the pilgrims as they arrive, circumambulate, pray, walk, run, sleep, pray, throw stones like they are supposed to, circumambulate again, pray again, buy gifts and return crowned with the newly acquired title of a *Haji* or *al-Haj*. Only the burning soul of Shariati can see in hajj the celebration of the monotheistic worldview, travel twenty-three years of the Prophet's life in twenty-three days' journey through Makkah and Madinah. In the resolve for hajj he sees dying before death; in *ihram*, the destruction of 'I' and 'me'; in the individual, he sees society and of society, he speaks of a single entity.

The emptiness of the Ka'bah frees him of the world of relativities and the 'House of God' appears to him as the 'Household of God', that is, the people. His dauntless mind connects Abraham's old age, Hagar's patience, the Ka'bah, her skirt, Safa and Marwah, Ishmael's thirst, her search and struggle and the miraculous Benevolence of *Zamzam* in one beautiful narrative of love between the Divine and His Slaves.

Every word of this narrative is an exegesis of God's abhorrence for falsehood and his nearness to the truthful, the dispossessed, the steadfast in faith. Arafah becomes knowledge; Mash'ar, sacred consciousness; and Mina, the station of love. The three *jamarat* become the three visages of Iblis: despotic coercion, exploitative wealth and deception masked by piety and buttressed by devious intellect. In the eternal confrontation among the three divine blessings and the evil triumvirate, Shariati sees an entire framework of revolutionary monotheistic movement. His observations on the last two *surah* of the Holy Quran (*al-falaq* and *al-nas*) and his moving explanation of the sacrifice of Ishmael are a befitting crescendo of this brilliant work—this lasting gift to the Muslims and all the dispossessed of the world.

For those who see Islam as a benign set of meaningless rituals, for whom *tawhid* perhaps is a mere numerical fact, who mechanically and habitually 'perform their ritual prayers', who 'slaughter' a lamb every year because they have to, for whom their 'Islamic practices' are a penance and retribution for realities of their otherwise materialistic lives, Shariati's *Hajj* will be too 'idealistic', perhaps even 'heretic'.

But for all those whose minds are thirsty and hearts forlorn in pursuit of Truth, this will come as a welcome rain shower. It is the most stirring invitation to all the Abrahamic nations of the world to resolve a return to their 'monotheistic home' by understanding their purpose and their station in the scheme of their Creator.

The Language of Shariati

The language of Truth is inherently convincing in its content and elegant in its form. Reading Shariati one cannot help but recognize that it is the prose-poetry that gushes forth from a spirit and an intellect that has been nourished with the power of the Quran and wisdom and eloquence of the Prophet. Divine in purpose, pure in content, elegant in that it is irreducible, and accessible to all, neither the words are exclusive and esoteric nor the construction forcibly philosophical and tedious. His words have the clarity of a brilliant dustless day. They flow like a torrential river and yet are calm, when needed, like a still lake. Shariati is poetic without being mystical. Ablaze like the desert wind as he speaks of tyranny and martyrdom, he becomes gentle as the morning breeze when in revere of love for the 'Ethiopian-slave' mother of Ishmael.

If one must describe his writing in stylistic terms, it is definitely exhortative, atmospheric and allegorical. Shariati's genius as a writer and a speaker lies in that he can take a subject that has been ignored as banal by the academics and render it so beautiful and eloquent that it becomes the very medium of convincing Truth. He has breathed life into the comatose visages of Islam. His language holds your spirit. It makes you run with it. It pauses and rests in a garden of contemplation. It then takes you into the most unfamiliar pathways of your dormant Muslim mind and it finally rewards you with insights and revelations that you never expected. Shariati is pure movement. His form, his content and his message are inseparable.

Having savored, in small portions, the Persian *Hajj*, I was awe-struck with the challenge faced by the translator. This *Hajj* in English captures with impressive honesty and finesse the emotions and eloquence of Shariati. I cannot imagine him speaking or writing in English any different than what you will find in the following pages. Through her translations, Laleh Bakhtiar has gifted Shariati to millions of human beings all over the world. Wherever this book travels so shall his spirit and his insuppressible message.

Sayyid Gulzar Haider
Ottawa, Canada
September, 1991

Notes to the Introduction

1. Muhammad Iqbal was born 60 years before Ali Shariati and died when Shariati was 5 years old. For Shariati's analysis of Allamah Iqbal's works see *Iqbal: Manifestation of the Islamic Spirit* which has been published jointly by ABJAD and Crescent International.

2. Murtaza Mutahhari was and, thorough his extensive expressions, continues to be one of the leading ideologists of the Islamic Revolution. He was martyred just a few months after the Revolution in 1979 by a member of the Furqan group. This group claimed to attach itself to Shariati's thoughts but in practice distorted aspects of Shariati which suited their own purposes. Clearly leftist *khawarij*, they took the criticism which Shariati directed at pseudo-religious scholars and the comments that he made calling for a reform among religious scholars and ulama to mean their total elimination. They began to carry out their treachery by martyring one of the dearest and clearest of the Revolution's teachers.

How strange that neither Shariati nor Mutahhari were to be present in the reconstruction after the Revolution that they had given their lives for. One died under mysterious circumstances of SAVAK's methods. How convenient it was for the enemies of the Revolution that Mutahhari was physically eliminated from the scene by a person who claimed that his bullet came from Shariati's thoughts!

But the lesson that the forces who work behind such treachery never seem to learn is that Truth persists. These two great men were Muslim *mujahid*s who stood in the same front. Although Mutahhari made some very strong criticism of some of Shariati's lectures, in particular, his very early ones, errors which Shariati himself had manly admitted to in his last will and testament when he asked that his brothers in faith correct any error he may have inadvertently made because he had been obliged by the circumstances of time and the pressure being applied against him by the security forces to state some things in great haste, yet Mutahhari was to write the following letter to Shariati just a few years before Shariati's death in 1977, a letter which clearly shows the love and respect that existed between these two social activists.

He wrote to Ali Shariati asking him to contribute to a book which the Husayniyah Irshad was preparing for the occasion of the passing of 14 centuries from the time that the Holy Prophet received the *ba'that*. The book is called: *Muhammad* (ص), *Khatam Payambaran*.

My dear brother scholar, Dr. Ali Shariati,

Your heart bears witness to the extent of my respect for you and what hope I hold for your future in enlightening the young generation to the truths of Islam. May God increase examples like you. I was anticipating a visit by you to Tehran before the month of Mehr (September 22- October 22) which would have gladdened the hearts of your sincere friends. Unfortunately your friends were not so rewarded. At any rate, we pray to God Almighty for your good health, felicity and further success.

Some time ago your honorable father and our dear master, Mr. Shariati, at my request, gave you a letter about the fact that upon the occasion of the end of 14 centuries after the *ba'that* of the Holy Prophet, a book is to be compiled with a great deal of care which will be useful in introducing the personality of the Holy Prophet. Our friends have divided it into roughly 20 topics, the list of which will be sent to you.

Three subjects relate to the history of the life of the Holy Prophet from birth to the *ba'that*, from the *ba'that* to the migration and from the migration to death, that is, it has been divided into three parts. Sayyid Ja'far Shahidi has agreed to write the first two, and, of course, he measures up to the task and the third part, which is more important than the first two, we request that you write. Perhaps the major and basic part of this book will be these three parts considering the *mujahid* and worthy authors. Clearly the third part will be longer. Although it has been agreed that the length of each part should not exceed thirty-forty pages but it is my opinion that the part which you are to write can be as long as fifty pages.

We anticipate that with your intuition, innovation and sense of selection, you will, in a succinct and, at the same time, clear way, present all of the illuminating parts of that aspect of the life of the Holy Prophet and, in particular, that, noting your clear perceptions, you will open up those parts which others have not attended to such as the causes which resulted in the migration and the benefits that Islam gained by the Holy Prophet creating a center outside Makkah and also the method of treatment of Islam and the Holy Prophet of peoples of other religious faiths, the method of rule and system of administering to Muslims from the political, social, and so forth points of view and the social training of Muslims, an analysis of the letters and messages of the Holy Prophet to the world's leaders of that day, and so forth.

I may possibly come to Mashhad in another two weeks and after spending one night there, I will journey to Fariman. I hope I will have the joy of seeing you. Please give my salams to all our friends.

Murtaza Mutahhari
(Persian printed in *Soroush Magazine*, vol. 3, no. 102, 1360/1981). [Ed.]

4. A *Husayniyah* is a traditional religious center where the people gather to see passion plays, in particular, those relating to the third Shi'ite Imam, Imam Husayn (ع) and his martyrdom at Karbala. The Husayniyah-i-Irshad mentioned here is located in Tehran. It is a center built in the late 60's and has extended the meaning to include a center for lectures about Islam. Ali Shariati was one of the first people to lecture there and drew crowds in the thousands. People gathered in the streets and surrounding areas to hear him. But as the Shah began to fear his effect, the secret police closed down the center for several years. [Ed.]

4. From the *Javid nameh* of Muhammad Iqbal. Translated by

Shaikh Mahmud Ahmad.

5. From *Asrar-i-khudi* of Muhammad Iqbal. Translated by R. A. Nicholson.

6. *The Reconstruction of Religious Thought in Islam*, p. 47. Shaikh Muhammad Ashraf, publishers, Lahore, 1960.

SHARIATI'S A WORD TO THE READER

I have arrived at the following conclusion in regard to history's religious missions and the course of historic change in religion in the name of a person knowledgeable about religion—as my speciality is History of Religions. I have done so with the dry eyes of science, as Francis Bacon would say, not with the tearful eyes of religious sensitivities or group prejudice. I have reached the conclusion by comparing that which has been to what it has become and then comparing the difference—the difference between the truth and reality of religions—with one another.

If we evaluate any religion from the point of view of the mission it bears for the salvation of humanity, I know of no mission more progressive in social growth, self-awareness, movement, responsibility, the seeking of human ideals, social insight, the spirit of longing for justice, the seeking of dignity, and, finally, tending towards reality, considering nature, being compatible

with material power and scientific progress, develop-
ment, civilization, the spirit of intellectual challenges, in
being oriented towards the people—and, at the same
time, more conscious and more powerful than the school
of Abrahamic monotheism as manifested in the prophetic mission of Muhammad, peace and the mercy of
God be upon him and his household. That is, Islam.
And, at the same time, I know of no mission which has
progressed to the extent Islam has towards degeneration. A comparison of what it was with what it has
become reflects the inconsistency.

If you were to compare the Islam of today with other
degenerate or degenerated religions of the world, you
might consider my judgment to be incorrect, but such a
comparison is not fair. The degree of the deviation of a
truth should be measured with that truth itself. It should
be evaluated in relation to its initial way and the beginning point of its movement.

If we turn ourselves to the task of studying Islamic
sects and evaluating them, using this method, we will
discover the fate of Shi'ism in Islam to be as Islam in
relation to other religions.

It is amazing!

In comparing the truth with the reality of other
religions, the word difference can be employed whereas,
in comparing the nature of Islam and Shi'ism with the
historic destiny of Islam and Shi'ism, such a word does
not do justice. Instead, the word contradiction is more
explicit.

And more amazing!

It is as if a power, having at its disposal all of the
hidden and often manifest, material, and spiritual pos-

sibilities, has assigned a group of the most powerful and elite philosophers of history—sociologists, anthropologists, philosophers, specialists in the human sciences, theologians, social psychologists, politicians, orientalists, Islamologists, Quranologists, jurisprudents, specialists in gnosis, and Islamic literature—to undertake a scientific study of Islamic culture and its people. They became familiar with the social mores, with the psychological and intellectual characteristics, and with the weak, sensitive and emotional aspects of Middle Eastern people. They studied the special tendencies of social and class behavior. They became aware of the role of celebrities, symbols, signs and powers among these masses and systems. This power, then, was given a profound understanding of Islam, in the most precise meaning possible of the word, by this group. They, then, reversed Islam, because it is clear that we are not looking at the natural degeneration and changes of a religion. What has occurred to Islam is a deliberate reversal.

It is so precise that it cannot have been simply an accident or something born from natural, unconscious elements in history. It is not just something resulting from a confrontation with foreign cultures, or influenced by tribal, class, and particular traditional perceptions of nations who joined Islam, or any other circumstances, conditions and historic, social, or cultural causes, which normally influence an intellectual school of thought or a religious faith, change, and divert it. It appears that this reversal in Islam has very consciously, maturely, and completely been made to occur so that the most progressive dimensions of its ideology or practice be changed into the most degenerated, anti-social elements.

It is interesting that it is here, also, that Shi'ism has been particularized by such a fate. It is obvious that two similar natures must have similar destinies. According to a more correct interpretation, just as Shi'ism is the most progressive manifestation of Islam's mission, it is quite natural, in such a reversal, that it be turned into its most degenerate, present manifestation [circa 1971].

As far as I understand, the most progressive dimensions of Islamic ideology or practice, which guarantee consciousness, liberty, movement, and the glory of its believers, and, more important than any of these, create social power, and responsibility are: monotheism, jihad and hajj.

Monotheism: We see that the teaching of monotheism ends in the schools of the traditional centers of learning. If any mention is made of it after this, it is only done by groups of sages and spiritual gnostics in their philosophical and subjective conversations, removed from life, and alien to the people. The emphasis is more on "proving the existence of God," and not that "God is One." In practical terms, they say: "We do not need to concern ourselves with monotheism. It is a subject which has been solved," and solved at the command of the enemy, or, at least, to his benefit!

Jihad: A forgotten word which has been left to history. Commanding to good or virtue and preventing evil or vice, *amr b'il ma'ruf wa nahy an al-munkar*, which is the philosophy behind *jihad*, has become a bludgeon for excommunication, not over the head of the enemy, but over the head of a friend, at that!

Hajj: The most illogical action which is repeated every year among Muslims!

And, in my view, the most progressive dimensions of ideology or practice particular to Shi'ism, which inspire the most sublime type of human leadership, a liberation-seeking spirit and revolutionary responsibility in Ali-like Muslims are: **imamate, ashura and anticipation.**

We see that the first, imamate or leadership, has become a means of recourse to omit one's duty. The second, *ashura*, the day of the martyrdom of Imam Husayn, has become the symbol of a school of bereavement! The third, anticipation, awaiting the Mahdi, has become a philosophy of submission, justifying oppression, and the tyranny of corruption, and condemning any steps for reform or any arisings for justice, before they even occur.

And they achieved all of these with a single policy—a policy which took the Book of Supplications from the cemetery to the city and the Holy Quran from life and the city to the cemetery where it was offered to the spirits of the dead. Taking the Holy Quran from their hands, it placed books on the Science of Principles at the disposal of the students of Islamic Science in the traditional centers of religious learning, who then put the Holy Quran on the shelf in their room. It is obvious that when the Quran not only deserts the life of Muslim people but Islam, as well, everything becomes possible in its absence and we see that everything has been done!

An intellectual feels responsible to his people; a Muslim to his faith. Thus, a Muslim intellectual, having a double responsibility, suffers both from the metamorphosis of the sublime values of his faith as well as from the degeneration of his people. His greatest anguish is to observe that his society—with the Christ-like spirit that it has which can give life to the dead and sight to the blind—is now so dying and becoming blind! What does he sense and what responsibility does he have to Islam and Muslim society? And, particularly, to the most developed, three-fold dimensions mentioned above of Islam and Shi'ism?

Can he remain silent? Is the treatment for the pain and the way of salvation of the people to take recourse in Western ideology? Can he negate, deny and disavow his responsibility and sit in fruitless anticipation for further centuries by using the excuse that it is religious scholars who are responsible for the destiny of Islam and only express his existence with intellectual grumblings? If Islam is a mission and not a special subject in philosophy or science, then it is only people who are directly addressed and it is a conscious clear-thinker who is directly responsible for it.

And you—my sympathetic intellectual, fellow Muslim: whether you consider yourself responsible to the people or to God, in practice, our work is the same, our responsibility, the same.

The course that our enemy has chosen for our humiliation is the best guide for us to choose as the way to our glory: Returning from the same way that he has led us. Bringing back the Quran from the cemetery to the city and its recitation, from now on, for the living! Bringing down the Quran from the shelf and opening it for our lessons.

They were not able to destroy the Quran so they

closed it, instead, and made the Book, a holy object. We should once again turn it into the Book and read it, for the word *quran* means just this.

Will the day come when we see the Quran has been accepted as a textbook in the Islamic programs of our traditional centers of religious training?

Will the day come when we see that the Quran must also be studied by students of religious jurisprudence as a religious textbook for achieving the level of *ijtihad*, that is, the level achieved after putting forth great endeavors in striving to understand religious issues?

If we bring back the Quran to our life and religion, then it will bring back monotheism to us as a worldview. Monotheism, hajj, jihad, leadership, martyrdom and anticipation will again find their life-spirit and we, also, our own spirit and life. And now, the hajj, a hajj in monotheism's worldview. And a hajj which is monotheism's worldview.

All the words I have to say about the hajj, the extracts of my deliberations and experiences during the three hajj's and one journey have been compiled in three volumes.

Twenty-three Years in Twenty-three Days
Volume One: Twenty-three Years in Twenty-three Days

It occurred to me that every pilgrim spends an average of twenty-three days in the peninsula for the hajj. For many years I have only thought about the Prophet and his life. Among all of our religious personalities, the Prophet is least known by us. If his life comes up occasionally, it is used to develop problems among the sects and theological, historical and ethical controversies between the Shi'ites and the Sunnis. As a result, only a few particular and limited examples of his instructive and amazing biography are repeated and even these few items mentioned are not based on research and independent investigation, but rather, upon fixed, prejudgments and one-sided, predetermined, imitative and, most often, prejudicial positionings.

Thus, for many years I have continuously been drowned in the astonishing personality, greatness of spirit and the allurements of the life of the Prophet. I have compiled the twenty-three years of the life of his mission—year by year in Makkah and month by month in Madinah. I have explored what I have read about the life of this great *ummi* Messenger of history in the geography of the land of the Prophet during my four consecutive journeys there. I have drawn the destiny of the Prophet upon the land of the Prophet.

I have drawn a map of the Arabian peninsula as it was during the age of the Prophet. I have indicated all of the tribes of that era on the present geographical map of the peninsula. I have also drawn the map of Makkah and Madinah during the age of the Prophet. I have specified the signs or traces of him and those of his family wherever they are to be found, friends and/or enemies who had dealings with him in Makkah, Madinah, Ta'if and the suburbs of Makkah, Ta'if and Madinah. I have pursued all of the courses of his journeys, battlefields and all traces of his life wherever he had lived or passed through.

In other words, I have located every place which had a trace of him in towns, mountains and deserts. I have precisely specified the battlefields of Badr, Uhud,

Khandaq, Bani Qarizah, Khaybar, Fath, Hunayn and Ta'if. I have prepared a perfect sketch of the Bani Hashim's area in Makkah and Madinah, the Prophet's mosque, the homes of each and every one of his wives, the home of Fatimah, peace be upon her, in Madinah, the home of Khadijah, Abu Talib, the birth place of Fatimah, peace be upon her, and the exact addresses of the eminent religious leaders and Companions as well as the area of his great enemies in Makkah so that one can find them in the greatly changed environmental situation of the Makkah, Madinah and Ta'if of today [1971]. One, then, can precisely visualize the town's environment and the social and family life of the Prophet. One can see living history, feel one's self to be part of the age, place and under the same conditions and states which have a close link with our soul.

Thus it is possible for you, the pilgrim, to be with the Prophet everywhere during these twenty-three days. Stay for thirteen days in Makkah, marking the thirteen years of stay there, and take a journey to Ta'if, following his way, a journey to invite and a journey to fight.

Migrate from Makkah to Madinah alongside the Emigrants. And, along the way, Rabadhah and Badr. Enter Quba. In Madinah, search every one of its streets and alleys, every one of the nodes which has a sign of him, his family and his Companions. Make a trip to Khaybar, this silent and virgin valley which has remained as it was fourteen centuries ago. See the castles of the Jews over the peaks of the surrounding mountains in the profound, mysterious silence of the damp, palm groves. Recognize every one of these. Listen to the thunder-like cry of Ali which still resonates in this memory-filled silence. See his signs with your own eyes. See the Marhab citadel upon the high peak. View other abandoned citadels, deserted houses and the silent, palm groves of Khaybar.

The detailed plans of the lines of battle scenes have been drawn where adventures were set down in the destinies of the lands of Badr, Uhud, Khaybar, Hunayn and Makkah.

Live with the Prophet for ten days in Madinah. Go everywhere he went and also find Ali and each and every Companion, even the homes of the Companions. See the old Madinah everywhere in the present Madinah. In this way, place yourself in the context of an ardent, loving, history of Islam, full of movement and jihad. Find yourself amidst the Emigrants and Helpers of the Prophet during those twenty-three years of the blessed history of human beings. See the history of Islam and the customs of the Prophet in this way, alongside the hajj. Learn of the complete, precise, living and determining course of Islam simultaneously with the hajj, in the cradle of Islam, in the dearest of lands and moments, in the most prepared of states and the freest time of life— which is normally futilely spent in useless expectations and more useless conversations, shopping and watching and discussing shopping.

The Appointment with Abraham
Volume Two: The Place of the Covenant with Abraham

Volume two is concerned with the meeting one has with Abraham. The discussion centers around Adam, Abraham, monotheism, the philosophy of history, the mission of Islam for humanity and the intellectual, historic, social, ethical or sociological role of monotheism, multitheism (*shirk*) and the basic scheme and philosophy of the hajj.

Rituals
Volume Three: Hajj: Reflections on its Rituals

Volume three, the present volume, concerns rituals (*manasik*). *Manasik* is the plural of *nusuk*. What meanings appear from the root *nusk*? Worship, devotedness, mortification and humility before God, whatever brings human beings closer to Him, everything one does for Him, washing and cleaning one's clothes, arriving at a destination, traversing the right path, taking the way of beauty and continuing to take it—every right which belongs to God, whatever is presented to God.

The *nasik* human being: a human being of pious devotion. A *nasik* land: a green and fresh land upon which rain has recently fallen. *Manasik*: a familiar and affectionate land, a region with which the heart is intimate and linked and the right path which God has placed before every *ummah* to walk upon in search of salvation and the truth! And *manasik*, rituals are neither solely contained in the treatises of religious jurisprudence or ceremonies and acts of the hajj, nor are they only contained in an intellectual treatise on the philosophy of these ceremonies and an interpretation and analysis of these acts. Rather, the special name of these ceremonies and acts in the hajj is 'rituals'. This is the name that Islam itself gives to them. It shows my interpretation of hajj, for I say the hajj is a combination of 'movements', 'orderly movements' connected to 'time' and in 'union', which accords with this nomenclature.

And this writing is an interpretation and analysis of this humble servant of God about these ceremonies and precepts. No Muslim has a duty to perform the ceremonies of the hajj according to this because this book is not a treatise of jurisprudence. It is a contemplative treatise. This is why I have only tried to interpret the rituals of the hajj. And not as a religious scholar, at that, or as an Islamic religious authority whose dictates are followed but rather as a Muslim pilgrim who, upon the return from the hajj, has the right to speak about it, about what was found there and speaks. And others, also, have the right to listen to one's words and they do listen.

This is not just a right but a custom, as well. Having gone on the hajj is itself an invitation to family, friends and neighbors to visit the haji so that, through this means, the issues of the hajj are made relevant every year. The gift the haji brings to his or her own land is an expression of what was understood in the place of the covenant with God and His people.

This is one of the great lessons of the hajj. Every year a minority, who were able, actually go and a majority, who were unable to go, participate in the hajj in theory. If those who are responsible to attend to food, hygiene, souvenirs and ugly, aristocratic extravagances and anti-hajj luxuries would give the same care, time and attention to training the million or so Muslims who undertake the hajj from the world over, from the remotest villages and the most primitive tribes and even if one thousandth of the fanaticism and stress on the analysis and compulsions are employed in the proper performance of its actions to express an understanding of the content of the hajj, the hajj would become a means of yearly instruction, a series of lessons whereby hundreds of thousands of free and enthusiastic representatives would be able, in one month, to become familiar with practical and theoretical Islamology, with the spirit of the hajj, with the mission of Islam, with the school of thought and action of monotheism and the fate of Muslim peoples. Then, with hand and heart full, they would return to their countries, their cities and environs of their work, life and faith and teach their own people that which has been learned.

In this way, the hajj will be like the roaring spring of Zamzam from which, each year, the Muslim *ummah* can quench its thirst by drinking of its thought and faith. A pilgrim will not just be one who 'kissed a stone' in allegiance but a bearer of light to people, a light which can illuminate the dark environment until the end of one's life. In this way, every person, at the level of one's own understanding, can, at least, when seated, familiarize the people around oneself, four hundred friends, family and fellow colleagues who come to visit, with the school of the hajj instead of recollections of repeated and nonsensical incidents and the vomitings of the journey.

Every year, all of the Muslims of the world would be trained through one million five hundred thousand teachers of the hajj and this Islamic tradition, whereby a Muslim must himself or herself invite people to visit, occurs twice:

Once, hajj and the other: death!

To think about the hajj, once a year, at a fixed time.

And to think about death!

Death, which has no time, death does not inform its victim.

But the victim of death informs you.

Beware!

Time! Time!

The hajj is exceptional among all of the other religious or non-religious precepts and acts.

The ritual prayer is the attraction of the spirit towards the spiritual center of the world, the great Deity and Beloved of Being, and, as Victor Hugo has said, "The One Who placed an infinitely tiny before an infinitely great."

This is a permanent, distinct concept in varying degrees, of course.

Jihad is an ideological war.

And, of course, the degree of understanding of this depends upon the depth of thought of the *mujahid*. This holds true for fasting and the poor-rate, as well.

But the hajj? Who can define it in one distinct term or phrase? What is the hajj?

The answer to this question is perhaps as varied as the number of pilgrims who think. The hajj—in whatever way it be understood—is a movement from self towards God, step by step with the people.

The hajj is an implicit rule, like implicit verses of the Holy Quran. Verses of the Quran are of two kinds: explicit and implicit.

Explicit verses are mono-dimensioned, words having a fixed, clear meaning. Implicit verses are multidimensioned, words that lead the mind to various meanings which can simultaneously be understood.

And the richest and most fundamental meanings are hidden in the content of the implicit ones. It is these verses, in every age, with every discovery, that open a door to the endless inwardnesses and with changes and transformations of thoughts and feelings, these complicated, intricate weaves, full of the mystery of expression, blossom still further and become more clear.

And it is in the heart of the mysterious oyster of these implicit verses where one must hunt and search for the diverse thoughts of future centuries which have remained concealed from the weak-sighted and slipshod thoughts of today and yesterday.

It is this hundred-fold, colorful kaleidoscope of implicit verses which has made the words of the Quran a simple message whereby a bedouin nomad can easily understand and discover that he is being addressed and, at the same time, a learned philosopher is amazed by its artistic miracle, spiritual richness and the depths of its intellectual complexities. Never does his searching mind nor his truth-seeking heart reach the end of it. It is these implicit verses which have guaranteed the perpetuity, effectiveness, learning and refreshing quality of this Book over the course of time—which erodes, ages, kills and gives birth to everything upon the earth—which is the place of being, annihilation, death and life.

Precepts are also like verses, in my mind, divided into explicit and implicit. *Jihad* is an explicit precept and the hajj is an implicit one!

And what has really caused difficulty in understanding these implicit precepts is that the language selected for their expression is a coded, and, in today's terms, symbolic one. And that which has added to its difficulty is that this symbolic language is not expressed through words but through movement, action. And a soundless movement: An implicit precept which has been expressed in a symbolic movement!

And in the hajj, it is not just language which has made it implicit, but the content, as well! Why so? Because the hajj is not so simple as to pour forth everything which exists in its heart to the sight of one generation in one era or open its inwardness to the needs of one understanding and the capacity of one feeling, and, in this way, become a repeated tradition, a solidified ceremony, a command which must be obeyed: absurd, hollow, spiritless, speechless, roleless, outdated, terminated and historic for other ages and for other generations.

Furthermore, the hajj does not set forth an ideology, a command or a value. The hajj is all of Islam. Islam in words is the Quran. In human beings, it is the Imam. And in movement or action, the hajj.

It seems as if everything which God wished to say to a humanity was spilled, all at once, into the hajj. It includes the philosophy of existence, a worldview of the philosophy of the creation of the human being and the course of history, in particular, the transformative phases of humanity—from the time of creation of mankind upon the earth, till the final peak of its perfection. It embodies what humanity must learn and the stages it must pass through in its servitude, in its ascent to the Summit and finally, the plan of creation for mankind's genesis, the formation of the *ummah*, model of humanity, the transformation towards perfection of the individual and the principles of eternal change, fixed order, precise coordination with time and social authenticity. In general: a consciously selected group movement towards Eternal Primordiality and Infinite Perfection:

God.

And the issue of guidance, ethical values, leadership,*ummah, maktab* (school of thought and action), historic connection, human society, cultural partnership, political solidarity, class, racial and ideological unity, way, movement, direction, goal, responsibility, ideology, self-sacrifice, fear of God, consciousness, self-awareness, mobilization, arms, preparation, weapons, strategy, *jihad,* martyrdom, love, blood, victory, freedom.

Everything ranging from the worldview of monotheism to the philosophy of existence to the struggle against war, discrimination and hunger!

Both God and bread.

Both servitude and salvation.

Both self-development and dissolution of the individual in the *ummah.*

Offer the 'self' to the people
Not for the sake of the 'self'
Not for the sake of the people
But for God!

*****

What have I understood from the hajj?

Before this question can be asked, another must be answered, that is: essentially what can be understood from the hajj?

The hajj, in a general view, is the existential course of a human being towards God. It is a symbolic drama of the philosophy of creation of the children of Adam. It is the objective embodiment of that which is relevant in this philosophy and, in a single word, the hajj is similar to creation and, at the same time, similar to history, and,

at the same time, similar to monotheism. It is at one and
the same time similar to *maktab*, similar to the *ummah*
and, finally, the hajj is a symbolic drama of the creation
of the human being and, also, of the *maktab* of Islam in
which God is the Director, the language of the play is
movement and the principal characters are: Adam, Abraham, Hagar and Iblis. Scenes take place in the sacred
area: the Masjid al-Haram, Mas'a, Arafah, Mash'ar and
Mina and the symbols: the Ka'bah, Safa and Marwah,
day and night, sunset and sunrise, idol and sacrifice.
Dress and ornaments: the *ihram*, *halq* and *taqsir*.

And the actors?

This is most amazing :

Only one person. You. Whosoever you are, whether
man or woman, whether old or young, whether black or
white, because you have participated in this scene, you
have the main role. In the character of Adam as well as
Abraham as well as Hagar and in the contradiction—
Allah/Iblis! For here no distinction is made and even
one's sex is not relevant. There is only one hero and that
is the human being! It is theater in which one person
plays all the roles, is the hero of the story and, at the same
time, the stage is open. Every year, all of the Abrahamic
human beings upon the earth are invited to participate
in this marvelous play!

Whosoever can arrive in season, from whatever part
of the world, enters the scene and undertakes the main
role, becomes the hero of the scene, plays all roles
oneself. There is no dispersion here, no distinction here,
no classification. All are one and that one, All. Islam
looks at human beings in this way!

"*Whoso slays a soul not to retaliate for a soul slain, nor for corruption done in the land, shall be as if he had slain mankind altogether; and whoso gives life to a soul, shall be as if he had given life to mankind altogether."* (5:32)

Is it not that a human being is a human being? Observe the value of a human being in this religion, yet its enemy accuses it of abasing the human being! This is a lie! The friend makes it into an instrument to abase the human being! This is the truth!

In our history—overflowing with oppression and suppression is anything more oppressed than Islam? And in Islam, than the hajj? As Ali, the son of the Ka'bah, so beautifully says, "The *poustin* of Islam is worn in reverse," and the same thing may be said of the hajj having become not the tradition of human beings but of sheep.

What have I understood from the hajj? It is so extensive that its meaning is endless, an infinitely great and what can an individual, this infinitely tiny, understand from that? What can be seen there? How?

My dear reader, this is the extent of my claim: if you want to know how to practice the hajj, read the treatises of the jurisprudents on the rituals. If you want to understand the meaning of the hajj, understand Islam and, within it, recognize the human being. And if you only want to know how I have understood the hajj, read this book. Perhaps reading it will stimulate you to understand the hajj, or, at least, in thinking a little about it.

A little.

Just this. Not more.

PART ONE:
THE SHORTER HAJJ
(umrah)

51—110

Hajj: resolve, intention. It means movement and includes the direction of movement, as well. Everything
will begin by digging 'you' out from the 'self', from your
life and from all your attachments. Are you not a resident in your city? Residency, repose. The hajj negates
repose, life, something the goal of which is itself. That is,
death. A kind of death which breathes. A living dead. A
corpse-like living, a slime-like being.

Hajj: flow!

Life is a rotating movement, a useless rotation, repetitious and futile comings and goings. The major task?
Growing old. The real consequence? Deterioration. A
monotonous and foolish fluctuation. A torture. Day, the
preliminary of night. Night, the preliminary of day.
Being occupied with cool and repetitive games of these
two black and white mice that gnaw on the thread of life,
shortening it until death.

Life? Watching. A watching of fruitless and senseless mornings and evenings. A flat and inconsequential game. When you do not have, all is anguish, endeavor and anticipation. When you find it and attain it, nothing—absurd, a futile philosophy, nihilism!

And the hajj? Your rebelling against this foolish determinism, this damned destiny. Turning away from vacillation, doubt, the rotation of life, production for consumption. Consumption for production.

Hajj unravels the skein of your being in which you have lost the thread of self. This closed circuit will open with a revolutionary intention. It will become a horizon. It will move on a straight course—migration towards eternity, towards another, towards 'Him'.

A migration from the house of 'self' to the House of God! To the house of the people! And you, whoever you may be—who are you? You have been a human being. You have been a child of Adam. But history, life and the anti-human social system has metamorphosized you. It has alienated you from your 'self', from your primordial nature. It has made you a stranger.

You were a human being in the world of particles. You were God's vice-gerent, a conversant with God, the special trustee of God, the Divine-like in nature, the Family of God. The Spirit of God had blown upon you. You were God's special pupil. God taught you all the Names. He taught you with the pen. God created you in His image. When God created you, He praised His power of creation. When He created you, He placed you erect. He cast down all of His angels, His angels near and far, before your feet. He brought everything into submission to you. He left the earth, heaven and everything in it to your mighty hands. He came to you and

Questions depressing answers

placed His special trust upon your shoulders. He made a covenant with you and placed you on earth. He Himself is within your primordial nature (*fitrah*). He became one within your house, then remained in anticipation to see what you would do.

And you? You took the path of history, setting off down the road, the knapsack of God's trust thrown over your shoulder: the covenant of God in your hand, the Names God taught you in your heart, the Spirit of God within your 'being-ness'. And time is your total capital and you, what is your work? Eating from your capital! Your life's profession? Being a loser. Not a loser of profits but of capital. Loss? And *"By the time, surely the human being is in the way of loss."* (103:1-2) Yet it is called living. And you, what have you done to this point? You have lived.

What do you have in hand?

The number of years you have lost.

And what have you become? O in the image of God! O responsible for His trust! O who the angels prostrated before! O vice-gerent of Allah upon the earth! In the world!

You have become money. You have become lust. You have become pot-bellied. You have become a lie, a beast, an animal. You have become hollow, absurd, empty! Or, no, full of muck and nothing else! For in the beginning you were a dead corpse. Mucky, putrid clay. God breathed His Spirit in this you. Where is that Spirit? That Divine Spirit, that Divine Soul? O muck-eating raven, emerge from this stilled marsh of self, from this swamp of your existence. Throw yourself suddenly upon the shore.

O putrid corpse? O corpse of slime! Desert this town, garden, village—mingled with disgrace. Head for the peninsula's desert, a sandy, blazing and dry desert under a heaven which rains down revelation. Face towards God. O dry, yellow, hollow cone! Moan from nostalgia, from exile and from alienation. O instrument of joy and happiness of strangers, enemies. O whose tunes are from the lips of others, seek out your own reed bed!

THE SEASON (*mu'sim*)

Now the time has ripened. It is the moment of meeting. It is the month of Dhihajjah, the month of the pilgrimage, the hajj, the month of reverence. Swords have been quieted. The neigh of the battle horses and the roar of the warriors and the brazen have grown silent in the desert. Fighting, avenging and fearing have given way to the earth for peace, worship and security. The masses have an appointment to meet with God. One should go in season. One must go with people to meet with God. Do you not hear the words to Abraham upon the earth: "*And proclaim the Hajj unto the people. They will come to you on foot and on lean camel, coming from every remote way.*" (22:27)

And you, O slime! Seek the Spirit of God. Return and ask for it from Him. Resolve to seek out His House from your house. He awaits you in His House. He calls loudly to you. Respond affirmatively to His invitation. Say, "*Here I am,*" (*labbayk*). And you, O who are nothing, you who are only a 'becoming' towards Him and that is all.

It is the season (*mu'sim*). Release yourself from this

filthy, disgraceful and humble, narrow life—this world. Save yourself from your suffocating and closed individuality—the ego. Resolve on Him with the sign of the eternal migration of the human being—the perpetual becoming of the human being towards God. Make the hajj!

Pay your debts. Wash away stains. Remove hatred. Make up with those with whom you have quarreled. Pay accounts. Seek the forgiveness of others. Clean the environment of your life, your links, wealth and savings. That is, you die here. It appears that you go, a going without a return. It is an allusion to the moment of the last farewell. It is a sign of the destiny of the human being. It is a drama of disconnecting everything to join eternity.

Thus: make your last will and testament which means death—a death which will forcibly select you one day. Now you make the hajj. Resolve on eternity, an appointment with God, the Day of Reckoning, where action is no longer possible, the time where your ears, your eyes and your heart are put on trial. They will, one by one, be asked: *"The hearing, the sight, the heart —all of these shall be questioned."* (17:36)

You, body, your body, you are responsible. All are responsible. And you, a helpless victim under the merciless, increasing attack of your deeds. Now that you are in the world of action, prepare yourself for the transfer to the world of reckoning. Practice dying. "Die before you die." Choose death. As a sign of death, choose death now. Intend death. Resolve death.

Make the hajj!

And the hajj, a sign of this return towards Him. He

Who is Eternal, He Who is Infinite, He Who has No End, No Limit, No Similarity.

To return to Him means moving towards Absolute Perfection, Absolute Good, Absolute Beauty, Power, Knowledge and Value. Truth means moving towards the Absolute. It means movement towards Absolute Perfection. That is, Eternal Movement.

This means that you are a perpetual becoming, an infinite movement. God is not your resting place. Rather God is your destination, a destination which will always remain a destination. God is not the final point in the course of your journey. Your journey, your eternal migration, is upon a road, a path which has no end point. It is a road which never ends. It is an absolute move. In this movement of yours in the world of being and in your own being, God is: eternal journeying and migration. Orientation, not place of stay.

Not Sufism! Dying in God and staying in God.

But Islam. Returning towards God. "*Surely we belong to God and unto God is the Return.*" (2:156) "*Unto God shall be returned all affairs.*" (42:53)

Not annihilation, but movement.

Not in Him but to Him. God is not far from you that you reach unto Him. God is closer to you than you.

To whom?

To you.

And He is farther away than to be reached.

By who? Anyone. Anything.

It is the season. Time has ripened. The time of meeting draws near. Go to the place of the covenant (*mi'ad*) at the appointed time— *miqat*! O you who have been called by God, it is time for the visit! It is the season. It is the appointed time.

O putrid clay. Visit with God.

You. O Family of God. You before whom the angels prostrated themselves. O human being, confidant of God. *"In a sure abode, in the presence of a King Omnipotent."* (54:55) History has metamorphosized you. Life has made you into a beast. O you who have made a a covenant with God to worship Him alone and to rebel against anything other than He, now you are the worshipper of the *taghut*—an arrogant, despotic ruler who rebels against God. You are the servant of idols! *"That which you yourselves carved."* (37:95)

O you who worship and pray to gods of the earth and not God of the Universe, God of the people, God of your own. O oppressor! O ignorant! O merchant of life, loser. The sacrifice of injustice and ignorance, loser to enslavement, abjectness, needs, the trampled upon by fear and greed!

O who life, society and history have made into a wolf or a fox or a rat or a lamb!

It is the season. Make the hajj! Go to the appointed time with the Great Friend of humanity. You have an appointment with He Who created you as a human being.

Flee from palaces of power, treasures of wealth, temples of deceit and degradation, from this herd of sheep whose shepherd is a wolf. Resolve to escape. Make the hajj to the House of God, the house of the people!

IHRAM AT THE
COVENANTED PLACE (*mi'ad*)
AT THE APPOINTED TIME (*miqat*)

The appointed time, the moment of the beginning of the drama. You who have resolved to meet God and who have now come to the place of the appointed time must change your clothes behind the scene of the drama.

Clothes? That which the you-ness of you, the your-ness of your being human has wound within it, worn; for clothes cover a person and what a great lie that a person wears clothes! The being human of a human is hidden. It shows itself off in the clothes of a wolf, fox, rat or lamb. Clothes are a fraud, a *kufr*, that is, the covering over of the truth.

The word clothes (*libas*) has a very meaningful sense, as well, which is understood in the verb form of *ifti'al*. *Iltibaz* means mistake! To make a mistake! Clothes are a sign, are a separation, a manifestation, a mystery, a degree, a title, a privilege. The color, design and quality of it all mean:

Me!

And me means not you. Not you. Not us. It means distinction and, therefore, discrimination. It means boundary and, thus, separation. And this 'me' is a race. It is a nation. It is a class. It is a group. It is a family. It is a degree. It is a situation. It is a value. It is an individual. It does not mean being human.

Boundaries are numerous in the land of humanity. The sharp blade of the three-fold executioners of history —the children of Cain—has fallen into the midst of the children of Adam and has, piece by piece, cut mankind's

unity into: master-servant, ruler-condemned, full-hun-
gry, rich-poor, master-slave, oppressor-oppressed,
colonialist-colonialized, exploiter-exploited, brain-
washer-brain washed, powerful-weak, wealthy-agent,
deceiver-deceived, aristocrat-abased, spiritual-physical,
noble-common, landlord-serf, employer-laborer, pros-
perous-wretched, white-black, eastern-western, civi-
lized-uncivilized, Arab-non-Arab.

Humanness has been divided up into races. Races
into nations. Nations into Classes. Classes into sects,
groups and families. Inside of each, again, position,
reputation, degrees and honorary titles exist. Bit by bit
they form an individual, a 'me' and all of these in
different clothes.

O actor! Throw them away at the appointed time.
Put on the shroud. Wash out all colors. Wear white.
Whiten and harmonize with all colors. Become all.
Emerge from your me-ness like a snake which sheds its
skin. Become the people.

Become a minute particle in mingling with other
particles, a drop lost in the sea. Do not be someone who
has come to the place of the covenant.

Become like a blade of grass which appears at the
appointed time.

Become a being who senses non-being or a non-
being who senses being. "Die before you die."

Take off life's clothes.

Put on the clothes of death.

Here is the place of the appointed time.

Whoever you are, throw away all ornaments, signs,
colors and patterns which the hand of life has clasped
over your body and has nourished you to become:

Wolf,

Fox,

Rat

Or lamb. Throw them all away at the appointed time.
Become human.

Be as you were in the beginning.

Be one.

Adam.

And as you will become in the end.

One—death.

Wear a two-piece cloth, one piece over your shoulder and one around your waist. A single color. White, unsewn, patternless, colorless, without any sign, without any indication that you are you, that you are not another.

At the place of the appointed time, the cloth worn by everyone, the cloth which you easily mistake with that of your companion.

Wear the cloth that you wear at the beginning of your journey towards God. Wear it now at the beginning of your journey towards the House of God.

Amazing! Here a noun of time has become a noun of place!

What does that mean?

It means there is also movement in a place.

That is, a place is also a movement.

That is, everything means time.

That is, place means time.

That is, never repose.

Yea. Is it not that a human being is not just 'being'? But is also becoming, a becoming towards God. *"Unto God is the ultimate return."* (24:42) Amazing! Everything is movement, perfection. Death and life. Life and death. Contradiction, change, direction! *"All things perish except His Face."* (35:18)

Everything is condemned to deterioration except what is turned towards Him.

And God? Absolute Being. Absolute Perfection. Absolute Eternity. The Absolute of Absolutes, too!

"Every day He is in a splendid manifestation." (55:29)

And the hajj? Movement. Resolving upon a destination.

The sign of the return of mankind towards God.

Dig the grave of all of your me-nesses in *miqat*. Bury your 'self' in it. Bear witness to your own death. Be the pilgrim to your own grave. Create the ultimate fate of your life with your own hands. Die in the place of the appointed time. Be resurrected in the desert between the place of the appointed time and the place of the appointment. It is the place of the Day of Judgment, where, from horizon to horizon, are the shrouded, an agitated flood of the white clothed, the people, all in a single color, single pattern, no one re-recognizing the other, therefore no one re-finding the self. The 'me' has been left behind in the place of the appointed time.

Now they are spirits who have been resurrected. They have taken on form, disregarding race, family, class, without name and without title. It is the place of resurrection, of blending together, of unity. A human manifestation of Divine Oneness, resurrection, fear, enthusiasm, excitement, astonishment, wonder and ecstasy!

Everyone is but a particle in the magnetic field of its givings and takings. God in the *qiblah*. Everybody is

nothing and only— human. All directions are eliminated except for orientation towards Him. All nations,
groups, humanity. The humanity of a tribe in the wilder-
ness, having one *qiblah* in existence, in life.

Take off your clothes. Desert all signs which distin-
guish you. Lose your self in the multitude of the gathering of the crowd of people. Forget whatever life has
attached to you. Whatever is a recollection of you.
Whatever tells of your system in the uproar of the
gathering of the people. Prohibit your 'self' all of these.

Wear the *ihram*. *Ihram*? To make sacred. It is an
infinitive used here as a noun and a noun for a kind of
dress.

All me's die in the place of the appointed time and all
become us.

Everyone sheds a skin and becomes human.

And you also bury your individuality and personality, become people, become the *ummah*. When you negate being 'me'—negate your 'self'—infiltrate into us.
Each person becomes a society. The individual becomes
an *ummah* as, "Verily, Abraham was an *ummah*." (16:120)
And you now go to become Abraham-like.

Everyone becomes the other. One becomes all and all
become one. The multitheistic society attains monotheism. It becomes an *ummah* and an *ummah* is a society
upon the way. *Umm* means resolve, movement towards
a destination, departure towards a *qiblah*, a gathering
not to be but to become, not for prosperity but for
perfection, not for tranquility, but for movement. As a
result, not management but leadership. Not rule but
leadership.

And now you and numerous you's and other me's.

What am I saying? Other nothings! From the four corners of the world, all turn from themselves and face
towards God. All turn away from the detention camps
of the world and face towards the Hereafter. All turn
away from relativities and expediencies and face towards the Absolute and the Truth. All turn away from
ignorance and tyranny and face consciousness and justice. And, finally, all turn away from multitheism, shirk
and face monotheism, *tawhid*.

You have arrived in the place of the appointed time.
You have put on the dress of the *ihram*. You will be
mistaken for others. It is a gathering. It is a resurrection.
Everyone takes a stranger as a friend and a foreigner in
place of a relative. Everyone wears each other's shoes.
Every *ihram* could be your *ihram*.

All of those who have for years forgotten their being
human, all of those who have become alienated by
coercion, wealth, position, land or blood, all of those
who have felt their cash on hand to be their 'self', who
have found their degrees and titles to be their 'self', have
now all become their true 'selves', their human self. All
have become one person—human being—and other
than that, nothing. All one adjective —haj—resolver—
and nothing more.

MAKING YOUR INTENTION KNOWN
(niyyah)

You are at the threshold of the entrance. You want to
begin. Before anything else, you must make your *niyyah*.
Niyyah? What does it mean? Intending to go some place?
Nawaka'llah, "May God be with you on your journey and

protect you." *Intawi*—move from place to place, to change from one state to another. *Nawan*—a traveler's destination. *Nib*—an old she-camel. *Niyaz*—granting needs. *Nawan*—date pits. Conceive your fruit. *Niyah*—destination, to stay. *Nawan*—remoteness, the distance the traveler has before him. Intention: resolution. *Niyata*—to be loyally attached to whatever is harmonic with itself. Need. Command. *Naw*—the person who intends to make the self ready for transformation, one who has in hand the belief of a group and the destiny of a society.

You are in the place of the appointed time, at the edge of a great change, a revolutionary alteration and transformation, a transition from your house to the house of the people, from living to love, from self to God, from slavery to freedom, from hypocrisy, deception, deceit, degree, position, class, race to truth and sincerity, from covered to uncovered, from daily clothes to the clothes of eternity, from the clothes of carelessness and recklessness to the clothes of self-sacrifice, commitment and the *ihram*.

Make your intention known, *niyyah.*, as a date whose seed conceives. O shell! O absurd! Plant the seed of that consciousness of self in your conscience. Fill your hollow innerness with it. Do not be just a body. Mature as the seed matures. Make your being a shell to surround the seed of your faith. Become a being. Be. Do not be a bubble. Kindle a flame in the darkness of your heart. Glow. Let your 'self' be filled. Overflow. Shine and let the radiance of Essence make you self-less and make you your 'self'. O totally ignorant, always inattentive. Become aware of God. Become aware of people. Become conscious of 'self'.

O you who have always been an instrument of labor.
O you who have always been obliged, selected by the
job. You have worked but as habit, custom, coercion.
Now make your intention known. Freely select consciousness of self. Do so knowingly, with awareness.

A new way.
A new direction.
A new job.
A new being.
And...a new self.

THE RITUAL PRAYER (*salat*)
IN THE COVENANTED PLACE (*mi'ad*)
AT THE APPOINTED TIME (*miqat*)

You are in *miqat*. You make your intention known
and begin the hajj. That is, you sense that which you
have begun. You are aware of what you are doing and
why you are doing it. You even remove your clothes.
You brush away your 'self', become uncovered and put
on the *ihram* and then stand for the ritual prayer. The
ritual prayer of the *ihram*.

Offer yourself in your new clothes to God. "Behold,
O God, I stand before Thee, no longer the slave of
Nimrod or the servant of the *taghut* but in the form of
Abraham. No longer in the clothes of coercion, a coercive wolf, deceitful fox, greedy rat, humiliated and
submissive lamb but in the clothes of a human being, in
the clothes I will wear to meet Thee tomorrow when I
shall rise from the dust."

This means: I am aware of my nature. I am nothing.
Rather, I am everything for I have become Thy servant

in obedience. I have become free through rebellion from everything and everybody other than Thee. I am aware of the point of the final destiny of my life. I now select myself whatever fate has prescribed for a human being. I practice it.

How amazing is this ritual prayer which means something else in *miqat*, in the white shroud of *ihram*, at the threshold of the place of the covenant! It is as if we hear new words. It is not the repetition of a religious ritual. We are speaking to Him. We feel the heaviness of His presence upon ourselves:

"O Merciful!," for Thou art caressing a friend! "O Compassionate," for the sun of Thy Mercy extends beyond the borders of *kufr* and faith, worthiness and unworthiness, purity and impurity and even friendship and animosity. Yea. I will praise no one but Thee for praise belongs to Thee. I will seek help from no power but Thee. O Thou Who art my only and sole Beloved. O Thou Who art my sole and only Helper. Guide all of us who have fallen into the waywardness of ignorance, who have not thrown away the misleadings of tyranny. We are the toys of our own weaknesses, the toys of powers other than Thee. Guide us upon the way of purity and awareness, truth and perfection, love and beauty. Join us to the group Thou hast loved and blessed with goodness and not those against whom Thou art angry nor those who have gone astray."

Every bowing (*ruku*) in *miqat*, in the white dress of Resurrection Day, *ihram*, is the denial of every time we bowed our head before any fear, greed or false deity. Every prostration (*sajdah*) is a denial of every forehead which we humbly put on the earth before a palace of power.

The ritual prayer in *miqat*. Every rising and every setting, a message, a covenant that from now onwards, "O God, no rising or setting will be done except for Thee and before Thee.

"Peace be upon you, O Muhammad, peace and the mercy of God be upon him and his household, His servant and Messenger! Peace and the blessings of God be upon you who granted such mercy and blessings to mankind within this life and upon this earth.

"Peace be upon us, upon the pious believers and good-doers of God.

"Peace be upon you..."

These words come to life there.

These pronouns all return to their origins.

All allusions are near.

There, all are present.

Nothing and no one is absent in the place of the appointed time: God, Abraham, the Prophet of Islam, people, spirit, resurrection, paradise, salvation, freedom and love.

And now you are clothed in the clothes of people, in the clothes of unity, colorless, patternless clothes. In white clothes, the clothes of piety and death, the clothes of rebirth. And, finally, the clothes of resurrection!

Ihram!

And you, O human being! Rejected of God! Plaything of Iblis! Exiled to the earth! Condemned to the strangeness, loneliness and anguish of the earth! Now you have returned in repentance and apology towards Him, in search of 'self'.

No longer remiss, but released, yet under an obligation, an obligation which you accepted of your own free will, at the height of your free choice and awareness, a pre-destination you yourself chose. Now you are bound to it. You are responsible. You are in *ihram*, in a sacred place. You are upon the way to the shrine (*haram*). You are upon the way to a sacred place at a sacred time and in the clothes of *ihram*. You are at the sacred boundaries of prohibitions.

What is *ihram*? To make sacred, to forbid.

Ihram? What things are forbidden in the state of sacred prohibitions? From what are you prohibited?

 PROHIBITIONS (*muharramat*)

Anything that recalls you to you are prohibitions (*muharamat*). Anything that distinguishes you from others. Anything that represents who you are in life and what you do. And, finally, anything which is a sign of you, a sign of your system of life, a sign of your social system. Whatever is reminiscent of the world, whatever you thought you could not leave behind. Whatever is not humane. Whatever recalls you to anything other than being a human being. Whatever reminds you of the usual day to day things. Whatever smells of your life prior to your *miqat*. Whatever leads you to your past, buried life:

1. Do not look in the mirror so that your eyes fall upon yourself. Let your 'self' be forgotten. Forget your being.

2. Do not use perfume. Do not smell good aromas, so your heart does not recall life's desires, so that desires do not arise within you, so that passions do not overtake

you, so that pleasures are not recalled to you. For here the environment is filled with another perfume. Breathe the fragrance of God. Let the fragrance of love intoxicate you.

3. Do not give orders to anyone. Enliven the sense of brotherhood. Practice equality.

4. Do not bring harm to any creature, not even the tiniest of insects. Bring no harm. Do not even expel by using force. Be like Christ for a few days in this world ruled by the system of Caesars.

5. Pull out no plant from the soil of the sacred area. Break nothing. Practice peace in relation to nature as well. Kill the nature of violence and destruction within yourself.

6. Do not hunt. Kill hard-heartedness within yourself.

7. Sexual intercourse is forbidden. Do not even look with desire so that love not spread itself upon your existence.

8. Do not marry. Do not partake in the marriage ceremonies of others.

9. Do not adorn yourself so that you may sense your 'self' as you really are.

10. Do not use abusive language. Do not debate. Tell no lie. Show no pride.

11. Wear no sewn clothes or clothes similar to ones that are sewn. Do not hold up your sacred clothes even with a thread so that all ways towards distinction in appearances be closed.

12. Take up no weapon but, if necessary, it should not show.

13. Shade not your head from the sun. To seek refuge

under a ceiling, an umbrella, inside a carriage or in a covered automobile is prohibited!

14. Cover not your feet with socks or shoes.

15. Adorn not and carry no adornments.

16. Cover not your head.

17. Cut not your hair.

18. Seek not the shade.

19. Cut not your nails.

20. Use no creams.

21. Bloody not your body or the body of others.

22. Extract no teeth.

23. Swear not upon God.

24. And, you, O woman! Cover not your face.

The hajj has commenced. Move towards the Ka'bah in the sacred clothes of *ihram* under the protection of prohibitions. Hasten towards God. Cry out, *"Labbayk! Labbayk!"* God has invited you. He has called for you to come. Now you have come. Now you respond to Him. *"Labbayk.* Yea O Lord. Yea. Praise and blessings belong to Thee and dominion! There is no partner for Thee. Yea."

Praise, blessings, dominion! Again negating the same three ruling powers: deception, exploitation and despotism, the trinity that has ruled over history: fox, rat and wolf, ruling over people who are all as lambs of God. The sound of God is heard in the desert. The call comes from every particle. It has filled the entire atmosphere between heaven and earth and all hear it as a call to them. They hear God calling them. They cry from the bottom of their hearts. *Labbayk, allahumma, labbayk.*

And you sense not your feet taking you forward for you are like a tiny particle of iron fillings which is attracted towards a powerful magnet. You are being carried forward. Your feet drag behind you. You sense your two arms are transformed into two strong wings. You are flying amidst a flock of white birds in space. You move towards the ascent, towards the Simurgh.

The Ka'bah grows close and closer. The excitement increases and becomes more agitated. You rightly hear your heart beat. It is as if a wounded and wild creature is within you beating its head against the wall of your very being, wanting to break out and run away! You feel you are growing larger than yourself. You sense you are overflowing. You no longer fit within your form nor within the pinching shoes upon the feet of your being nor within the tight clothes upon the body of your existence. Tears cannot be restrained. It is as if little by little you sink into a space filled with God.

This presence upon your skin, upon your heart, upon your intellect, in the depths of your primordial nature, in the reflected light of each piece of gravel, on the face of every rock, at the mid part of every mountain in the far ambiguity of every horizon in the depth of the desert. You see only Him. You find only Him. Only He exists. Other than He, all is wave, foam—lie.

Love rains upon the desert and dampens the earth.

And whereas the feet of a man sink into mud, your feet enter love.

You move and sense your own annihilation. You move away from 'self' and near to Him. All become He and you become Him. All and you, nothing —a forgotten memory—which fell off your shoulders in *miqat*. And you, lightened of the burden of self, move towards the place of the covenant. You sense you no longer exist.

A particle of ardency is all that is left. Nothing more. You are only a movement. You are only a direction. You move forward having no right to step back. You face Him. You vanish in Him like a part of a cloud sucked up by the desert sun.

The heart of existence pulsates and space overflows with God. You have overflowed from God.

Love rains upon the desert and dampens the earth.

And whereas the feet of a man sink into mud, your feet enter love.

You arrive at the outskirts of Makkah. The city is near. You reach a sign here, a sign which says, "This is the boundary of the sacred area." Makkah is a sacred area. In this area, war and aggression are forbidden. Whosoever escapes from the enemy and takes refuge in the sacred area is immune from pursuance. The hunting and killing of animals and even the pulling up of plants from the earth is forbidden here.

After the attack of the Prophet upon Makkah to free the Ka'bah from idol-worship, the Prophet himself, with his own hands, once again marked off this area. He strengthened the old tradition to preserve the sacred area, to prohibit aggression and murder in this area.

You pass this border and now you enter the sacred area. Suddenly the tumultuous cries of *"Labbayk"* which have reached their peak, cease.

Silence.

That is, "You have arrived."

He Who calls you is here. You have reached His House. Silence!

A silence in His Presence, in the sacred area, the sacred area of God.

You move forward. The desire for the Ka'bah is oppressive.

But first, the city.

Like a large bowl, all of its surrounding walls— mountains. Every one of its streets, alleys and lanes—a valley, a fissure in the mountain, a cut-away, from all directions pouring down towards the base of this great mountainous nest. Here is the sacred mosque: the Masjid al-Haram and in the center of it, the Ka'bah!

You pass through the mountainous spirals of the town. Step by step you move closer to the Ka'bah. You pour down like a flood and the nameless, the undistinguished flow onto the bed of the valley. A street, towards the depth of the valley, the Masjid al-Haram. It flows and you, a drop!

Step by step you descend. Step by step its greatness nears. In the words of an awakened, sensitive sympathizer, "We always have the habit of climbing upwards, of moving towards heights and loftiness to reach greatness, in particular when greatness is Divine, when words are about the Divine angelic world and here, the opposite. However much you descend from peaks, however much you come down from the heights, you grow closer to God!"

Does it mean that through humility and humbleness you reach greatness and majesty? Attaining great heights through servitude? That is, do not search for God in the heavens, in the meta, but upon this very earth, upon this inferior soil, in the depths of the material of a stone. You can find Him, see Him. You must find the Way correctly. You must learn how to see correctly and perhaps, a secret of the fate of mankind—descending into the dust and arising before God!

The Ka'bah is close by. Silence. Contemplation. Love.

Each step is more tumultuous. Each breath more fearful. Moment by moment, the weight of His presence, heavier. You dare not blink your eyes. Your breath does not come easily. You are nailed to your vehicle. In a state of silence from head to toe, perplexed, ardent, leaning a little forward, all your body—eyes. You only look forward. In front, opposite you, the *qiblah*. How heavy is the weight of bearing the anticipation of the visit. How difficult is the anticipation of seeing such greatness. How can the thin walls of your feelings and the unsure veil of your heart bear it all?

You find your way down through the twists and turns of the valley. At every curve you pass, your heart leaps. Now the Ka'bah? The Ka'bah, this *qiblah* of existence, faith, love. The direction for our daily and nightly ritual prayers. Towards it we pray every morning, noon, afternoon, evening and night. We die facing it. We are buried facing it. Our home, our grave and now, only a few steps away from it and in a few moments, before it, before my sight:

THE KA'BAH

You are at the threshold of the Masjid al-Haram. Now the Ka'bah before you! An enormous courtyard and in the center, a hollow cube. Nothing more! You suddenly tremble! Wonder, amazement! Here, there is no one. Here, there is nothing. Nothing to even see.

An empty room, that is all.

Your senses are fixed on a bridge, thinner than a

strand of hair, sharper than the edge of a sharp sword. Is the *qiblah* of our faith, our love, our ritual prayer, our life and our death just this? A pile of dark, rough stones, placed upon each other, spaces unevenly and inexperiencedly filled between with mortar, nothing more!

Suddenly a doubt runs through you.

Where is this? Where have I come? I understand a palace or the beauty of an artistic architecture or a temple. I understand a sacred magnificence and spiritual silence under high, grand, elegant, artistic ceilings. I understand a tomb—the burial place of a great person, a heroic genius, Prophet, Imam!

But this? In the midst of an uncovered area, an empty room! No architecture, no art, no beauty, no inscription, no tile, no plaster-moulding, not even the burial place of a Prophet, an Imam or a grave of an eminent person to whom I can pilgrimage to recall the person that I had come to see so that I can feel a point, a visage, a reality, an object. And, finally, a person, thing, place. Sit and relate.

There is nothing here. There is no one here.

Suddenly you understand how good it is that no one is here! No phenomenon draws your attention. Suddenly you feel the Ka'bah is a roof, a roof from which to ascend, to suddenly leave the Ka'bah behind and open your wings in space. Then you feel absoluteness!

You sense eternity.

That which you never sensed in your divided life, that which you do not find in your world of relativities, that which you cannot feel, you can only philosophize about, can be seen here: absoluteness, eternity, non-direction.

He!

How good that there is no one here. How good it is that the Ka'bah is empty. You gradually realize you did not come to visit a shrine. You have made the hajj. This is not your final destination. The Ka'bah is a sign so the way is not lost. It is only a sign, an arrow. It only shows you direction. You have made the hajj. You have made the resolution, resolved upon the absolute, moving towards eternity, eternal motion, towards Him. Not the Ka'bah. The Ka'bah is not the end of the Way. It is the beginning! Here the end is your own disability, death and your stopping. That which exists here is movement, direction and nothing else.

Here is the place of the covenant, the meeting place of God, Abraham, the Prophet of Islam and people! And you? As long as you are you, you are absent here. Become people. You who are wearing the cloth of the people, the people are the beloved of God. They are the Family of God. God is more zealous of His Family than anyone else. And here, His sacred area, within His sanctuary, His House. *"This is the house of the people. Verily the First House made for the people is the one at Makkah, blessed, and a Guidance for (the people) of the world."* (3:96)

And as long as you remain you, there is no place for you in the sacred area.

This is the *bayt al-'atiq. Atiq* comes from the root *'itq* meaning to free a slave. *Atiq,* freed! A house which is free from private ownership, the reign of tyrants and rulers. No one has power over it. The owner of the House is God and the household, the people.

When you travel 48 kilometers from your home,

town or village, you are a traveler and recite a partial ritual prayer, the ritual prayer of a traveler and yet, here, regardless of which corner of the world you have come from, you may recite your prayers in full because you are not a traveler. You have returned to your residence, your town, place, secure, your house. You were a stranger in your country. You were a traveler. Here, O reed torn from its rushy bed! O exile upon the earth! Human being: you have returned to your rushy bed, to your real birthplace.

God and His Family. People, this beloved Family of the world now in their house and you, as long as you are you, are a stranger, without connection, cut off, without refuge, a homeless being. Leave you-ness. Leave self outside. Enter the house. Join the Family. If you have buried yourself in *miqat*, if you have become the people, here, like a relative, friend, close relation, as one of God's Family, you will have entered the House. You will see Abraham at the threshold, this old rebel against history and this denier of all earthly lords, this great lover, humble servant of the God of monotheism.

He laid the foundation of this House with his two hands.

The Ka'bah upon the earth, a secret of God in the universe.

What is it constructed of? How is it decorated? How is it ornamented?

Pieces of dark stones which were cut from Mount 'Ajun near Makkah, laid down simply, one upon another, without any art, special technique or decoration, that is all!

And what is its name, its properties, its titles?

Ka'bah.

A cube. That is all!

Why a cube? Why so simple, without distinction or ornament? God is shapeless, colorless, without similarity. Whatever form or condition mankind selects, sees or imagines is not God.

God is Absolute.

Is without direction.

It is you who take direction before Him.

This is why you direct yourself to the Ka'bah and the Ka'bah itself is directionless. The thoughts of a person cannot conceive of non-direction. Why? Whatever you imagine to be a mystery of His Existence—absolute non-direction—of necessity, you assume a direction. This is not the mystery of God.

How can non-direction be revealed upon the earth?

In this way only—all opposing directions be gathered together.

So that each direction is negated by its opposing side. Then only does the mind understand non-direction.

How many directions are there?

Six.

What form contains these six directions?

The cube!

Its exact secret?

The Ka'bah.

"Therefore, wherever you turn, there is the Face of God." (2:115)

Because of this, inside the Ka'bah, whatever direction you wish to face for the ritual prayer, you face Him and outside the Ka'bah, which ever way you face, you face Him.

What other form—except the cube—faces north, south, east or west, towards the earth or towards the heavens. The Ka'bah faces all, faces none, everywhere and nowhere, all directions and, yet, no direction. God!

His mystery: the Ka'bah!

But wonder! To the west of the Ka'bah is an addition, changing its shape and giving a direction to it.

What is this?

A short, arched wall facing the Ka'bah.

What is it named?

The *hijr* of Ishmael!

Hijr? What does that mean?

Skirt! And it actually resembles a skirt. The skirt of a dress, the dress of a woman!

Yea.

An Ethiopian woman.

A slave!

A black slave.

The slave of another woman!

A slave, so humble, that the other woman chose her as her husband's mistress. That is, she was so abased that she will never be considered as being a rival wife.

And her husband slept with her for her to bear a child.

A woman who in human systems lacked every dignity, every honor, and then God united the mystery of her skirt with the mystery of His existence.

This is the skirt of Hagar's dress!

The skirt which nourished Ishmael.

Here is Hagar's home.

Hagar is buried near the third pillar of the Ka'bah.

Amazing! No one, not even a Prophet should be

buried in the mosque.

And here, the House of God, wall to wall with the house of a female slave.

And the House of God, the burial place of a mother. What am I saying?

God's non-direction is only directed from her skirt! The Ka'bah has extended towards her! There is only a small space between this arch and the house. One can pass through this space when circling the House.

But circling around the Ka'bah, the mystery of monotheism, without circling around her skirt is not accepted.

It is not a hajj.

It is a command. A Command of God.

All of humanity, in the always of the ages, all who believe in monotheism, all who have accepted God's invitation, should, in their circumambulation of love around God, around the Ka'bah, circumambulate around the skirt of her dress as well.

Her house, her grave, her skirt, also, are part of the circumambulation, are a part annexed to the Ka'bah.

For the Ka'bah, this absolute, non-direction is only directed towards this skirt.

The Ka'bah is directed towards the skirt of an African slave, a good mother. The perpetual place of circumambulation of humanity.

The God of monotheism, seated alone upon His Omnipotent Throne, rejecting all galaxies behind Him, beyond everything which exists, He is Alone, and, in His heavenly kingdom, Unique.

But it seems as if from among all His creatures, in His infinite Creation, He selected one.

The noblest of His creatures, the human being.
And among all? A woman.
And among all?
A black woman.
And among all?
A black slave woman.
And among all?
A black female slave of a woman.
The most humiliated of His creatures!

[handwritten margin note: concurrent w/ the idea that islam is equality]

He has placed her beside Himself, a place beside His House.

Becomes her neighbor.
And now
Under the roof of this House, two:
One, God,
And the other, Hagar.

The unknown soldier has been so chosen in the nation of monotheism.

All of the hajj is joined to the memory of Hagar.

And *hijrah* or migration, the greatest deed, the greatest command is derived from the word *hajar.*

And *muhajir* or migrator, the greatest Divine-like human being, a Hagar-like person.

And what is migration?

A Hagar-like deed. In Islam, it is to go from savageness towards civilization and this journey means to move from *kufr* to Islam because *t'arub ba'd al-hijrat,* in the language of people, means savagery after becoming civilized. In the words of Islam, it means to return to *kufr* after having found faith. Thus, *kufr* means savagery and religion means civilization.

And *hjr,* an Ethiopian word means town or city in the

language of Hagar and Hagar, a black African, Ethiopian slave woman.

The manifestation of a pre-civilization human being and yet, here, the root of civilization. Thus, a Hagar-like human being means a civilized one. A Hagar-like movement means the movement of humanity towards civilization.

And now, in the movement of humanity around God's House, again, Hagar. Your place of circumambulation, O migrator who has resolved on God, is the Ka'bah of God and the skirt of Hagar.

What do we see?

Our understanding cannot contain it!

The sensitivities of a human being in the age of liberation and humanism have not the power to bear this meaning!

God in the house of a black, African, female slave.

CIRCUMAMBULATION (*tawaf*)

Now, this is the Ka'bah, in the midst of a whirlpool, a roaring whirlpool which whirls around and circumambulates the Ka'bah, a constant point in the center, and other than this, everything moves in its surroundings, circle-like around it.

Eternal constancy and eternal movement!

A sun in the center and around it, each one, a star, in their sphere, circling around the sun.

Constancy, movement and harmony: circumambulation.

An imagination of a solar system? Or the incarnation of all of the world? In the worldview of monotheism?

God is the Heart of the universe. He is the Axis of existence. He is the Center of the universe which everything circumambulates around and you, in this system, whether in the Ka'bah or the universe, are a particle, a particle in movement and each movement, in a place. You are a continuous movement. Just a state and with each breath, a state constantly in change, in becoming, in circumambulation but always and everywhere your distance from Him and the Ka'bah, constant. There your nearness and farness relates to what ray you have selected in this rotating circle. Whether near or far, you never touch the Ka'bah, never stop by the Ka'bah for there is no pausing because for you there is no constancy, there is no unity of being. Monotheism exists. The whirlpool of human beings rotates around the Ka'bah and that which can be seen is only the human being. It is here that you can see the people and not see man or woman, not see this nor that, me nor him nor you nor them. See universals, not particulars for the individual has been dissolved in the totality of human beings. It is the annihilation of the individual but not in God. Rather in us, in the human being, in people. It is better to say: in the *ummah*! But annihilation in the direction of God, for God, in the circumambulation of God.

It means the annihilation of the individual in people, the survival of the individual in the people. For God and the people are in one orientation, are of one rank. That is, here the way is towards God, passes through the people, from individuality to aloneness. Here is no Way to there. Your monasticism is not in a monastery but is in society. Self-sacrifice, sincerity, self-negation, bearing bondages, deprivations, tortures, anguishes and accepting dangers in the arenas of clashes and for the sake of people that you reach God. The Prophet has said, "Every religion has a kind of monasticism and the monasticism of my religion is *jihad*."

It is because of this that in circumambulating, you should not turn towards the Ka'bah or enter inside the Ka'bah. Neither should you sit or stand in the Ka'bah. You must enter the group, vanish in the circumambulaters, drown in this human whirlpool. It is in giving of what one oneself needs, self-sacrifice, *ithar*, in leaving the self among the circumambulating masses and in joining the congregation that you make the hajj, become a haj, respond to God's invitation with *labbayk*, find your way to God's sanctuary.

What do you see? The Ka'bah standing. And surrounding it? A white, uniform, single-colored, single-patterned flood, bearing no distinctions, no signs nor symbols, giving no superiority to any individual. No one can be distinguished. It is only here that you see universality with your own eyes.

Outside the Ka'bah the individual is a reality, a particular, is an objective, the universal of a subjective concept. The human being is a meaning, an idea, an intellectual, subjective and logical concept. In the external world, there are only human beings and whoever exists is either Hasan or Husayn, is a man or a woman, is an Easterner or a Westerner. Here all realities have been effaced. A universal concept, intellectual or subjective truth has found external, objective reality. Now it is only human beings who circumambulate the Ka'bah— only people and no one else.

And you, as long as you remain you, you remain outside the circumambulation. You stand still as an observer on the shore of this whirlpool of humanity. You stand still! Therefore you are not. Therefore you are a stranger. You are an individual, a nothing, a particle of a galaxy which has been thrown into space and disappears. You must come into being. Here they teach you that only in the negation of self will you attain proof. Slowly but surely, sacrificing yourself to others, to the *ummah*, will you, little by little, bit by bit, achieve self. Only then will you discover self and realize the true Self. Then, when in self, suddenly, in a revolutionary way, in giving over to death, you will be annihilated in a red death so that when you achieve martyrdom, you become a witness. Martyrdom (*shahadat*) means presence, means life, means whatever or whoever is perpetually present, is perceptible. A martyr is one who perpetually exists, is present, an observer, a visible and objective example, an eternal, living being!

"Reckon not those who were slain upon God's Way to be dead. Nay, they are alive with their Lord, by Him provided." (3:169)

Upon God's Way means the way of the masses. Both are the same. There is no way from individuality to Allah. If you ask, "Then why individual worship?" In order to develop the self, to nourish the self, to reach the threshold of *ithar*, self-sacrifice, to find the merit of putting aside self-interests for the congregation so that you become a human being. When the individual is annihilated, the human being remains. The human being is God's vice-gerent in nature as long as God is God. The human being is His vice-gerent, is His Shadow, is

His Sign, that is, is human. In this eternal dying to self, you are reborn and will remain eternally. A drop isolated from the sea is dew which lives only one night. Its life is just one night. It is a resident which vanishes with the first smile of light.

But it is in joining the stream that you become eternal, find flow to attain the sea.

Why are you standing still? O dew! Beside the fine, rhythmic, wavy whirlpool which harmoniously narrates the story of Creation's system, join the whirlpool. Step forward.

Now you want to join the people. You must make your intention known to become conscious. To know what you are doing, to know why you are doing it. For God, not self. For Truth, not expediency!

For here every action has a reckoning. A precise system governs this continuous movement for the universe is so.

THE BLACK STONE (*hajar al-aswad*) AND THE OATH OF ALLEGIANCE (*bayat*)

Enter the circumambulation from the corner at the Black Stone (*hajar al-aswad*). It is here that you join the system of the universe. You join the people in the whirlpool of the masses. You vanish like a drop and you remain. You find your sphere. You begin your movement. You are placed in a circuit. In the circuit of God but in the course of the masses.

You must begin by touching the Black Stone. Touch it with your right hand and, without hesitation, give yourself over to the whirlpool.

This stone is a mystery of the hand, a right hand. Whose hand? The Right Hand of God. "The Black Stone is the Right Hand of God upon the earth."

A lone individual, in order to live, or a lone tribe, in order to have support in the desert, concludes a treaty of friendship and mutual support with a chief of a tribe, with the tribes and forms a confederation with them. People conclude a treaty with a leader for a goal. This treaty is called a *bayat* or allegiance. Its form?

When you form an allegiance with a leader, head of a tribe, you extend your right hand and he places his right hand on yours and in this way you agree together and become allies.

And it was the custom that when you placed your hand within the hand of another in allegiance, you were freed of all previous allegiances. And now the moment of choice is here, choosing your way, your goal and destiny at the beginning of the movement, at the threshold of departure from self and being drowned in others, joining people and becoming harmonious with the congregation. You must give your allegiance to God. God has stretched out His Hand to you. Extend your right hand. Ally yourself with Him. Become His ally. Break all previous treaties and ties. Break your alliances with coercion, wealth and deception. Break your treaties with the lords of the earth, heads of tribes, the aristocratic Quraysh, masters of houses. Leave aside everything. Be freed.

"The Hand of God is above their hands." (48:10)

Sense the Hand of God upon yours. Caress it. This Hand is above their hands —those who tied your hands in their allegiance.

You are freed from allegiance to others. You have given your hand to God. You have renewed the covenant of your *fitrat* (primordial nature). You have become responsible and an ally of God! Join the masses. Do not stand still. Move. Find your circuit. Select. Give your self to the congregation. This is circumambulation. Enter.

Like a brook which joins a great and powerful river, step by step, you grow distant from your still and separate self. You join the congregation. You circle and endeavor for the ray of your circumambulating circle to grow closer to the House. You sense that you do not go alone but move with the congregation. Little by little, you sense you do not move. It is the congregation that takes you. Your feet, which have always supported your individuality, are being released and are out of work. The power of the congregation, the movement of the congregation, the endeavor of the congregation, the allure of the congregation, the beloveds of the world, have tightly embraced you. You are no longer on your own two feet. You are now under the control of others. You do not exist. Only the congregation exists. The more you move to the inside, the more the pressure of the congregation increases. It presses itself upon you. The congregation cannot bear you who still have me-ness. It destroys you. It magnetizes you. It digests you in the eternal, living, moving body of the congregation: people, human being. You are a drop of blood, living, eternal.

Flowing, not by self but in congregation.

And you join the congregation.

Not as an expediency but for love.

And see the God of Abraham. The connection of a servant with Self is found in the connection of the individual with the congregation. How subtle, beautiful and deep! He allures you to the congregation with the love of Self. You have come to visit God and you find yourself in the midst of the commotion of the masses. He has called you to His House, to the solitude of His visit. Now you have come all this way and He says to you: join the congregation. Go with the congregation. Do not enter the inside of the House. Do not stand beside the House. Do not even face towards the House. Do not circumambulate facing the House. Move shoulder to shoulder with the congregation. Face forward. The Ka'bah is the *qiblah* and in the circumambulation, if you leave the circuit and face the *qiblah*, you have wasted the circumambulation. Do not hesitate. Do not go left or right. Do not turn back. Do not turn your head back. You are beside the Ka'bah. Do not look at the *qiblah* because the *qiblah* is before you.

Now you have become part of the order of creation. You have been located in the circuit of this system. You have entered the gravity of the sun of the universe and, like a star, from left to right, you are circumambulating around God. You whirl and whirl and little by little you sense that you are nothing. You do not recollect your self. You do not recognize your self. Only love and the allurements of love exist. You are magnetized.

You whirl and whirl and nothing exists. There is only He and you are a non-being, a non-being who senses being or an existence who senses non-being. You whirl and whirl and feel that you are a point, that you had previously been a point and in this circumambulation, you, you become a continuous line, a circuit. You are only a movement. You are a circumambulation. You are a haj. His circumambulation, His hajj and you, a submission. You are a trustee, a bestowed upon. Higher than freedom, you are a predeterminism which you yourself have chosen.

Love has reached its peak. Love has reached towards the Absolute and you from your self. You have substracted your self. You have become singular. You realize that little by little you melt in Him. Little by little you vanish in Him. You become head to toe, love, sacrificed.

If love is to be described with movement, how would this movement be?

The butterfly has taught us long ago.

The Ka'bah is the center of love. You are the point of a compass, wandering in this circle.

Hagar has taught us.

The great Beloved, the great Ally of human beings— God orders her: "Take your nursing child. Migrate from the city, land and cultivation. Move to this frightening valley," where even a plant, a thistle, is afraid to appear. She fully surrenders and carries out the Command, the Command which only love can accept and only love can understand.

A woman alone. A child alone. In the depths of a distant valley. In the midst of these dry, burned out, stern mountains where the stones are all solidified lava.

How is it possible without water? Without habitation? With nobody around?

But...He has so Commanded. He has so desired. Trust in Him. Absolute trust. That which intellect, reasoning and logic cannot understand. Life needs water. A child, milk. A human being, a companion. A woman, a guardian. A mother, a supporter. Alone, a friend. And weak, a helper.

Yea. But love can replace all these non-availabilities. One can live with love if the spirit recognizes love. One can fight with empty hands if a *mujahid* is armed with love. O lonely, weak female slave, child, mother, lean on Him. Secure your life with love, trust.

At the end of the seventh circle, leave the circumambulation.

Seven? Yea.

Here seven is not six plus one. It means, "My circumambulation around God. My self-sacrifice to the masses is everlasting, is infinite."

Continuously circle Him in the way of the masses. It is the hajj, not a visit to a shrine.

Seven recalls the creation of the universe.

And you, in circumambulation, do you not find yourself a particle from the universe? Is not circumambulation around a center, a drama of existence?

The worldview of monotheism, its interpretation through movement.

And now the two cycle ritual prayer here, in the Station of Abraham.

Where is this? The Station of Abraham? A piece of stone with two footprints, the footprints of Abraham. Abraham stood upon this stone and laid the Black Stone of the Ka'bah in place.

He had stood on this stone and had built the Ka'bah.

It shakes you up! Do you understand? It means putting your feet in place of those of Abraham. Who? You.

Ah, what this monotheism does to a person! How difficult it is. Sometimes it makes you nothing and sometimes it makes you everything. Sometimes it does not bear your being you. Sometimes it pulls you to putrid clay. Sometimes it elevates you to the heights of the Divine World so that you kneel, knee to knee, before God. It takes you to the solitary sanctuary of God. It calls you a member of the Divine Family. It sees you as the vice-gerent of God.

It beats you, pounds you, negates you, dissolves you. It annihilates you. It belittles you . It makes you bend your head in servitude. It causes you to place your forehead on the earth in prostration and then it calls to you:

"O friend! O beloved! O companion of My solitude, confident of My sanctuary, My mysteries, bearer of My trust, My audience, Goal of My creation, companion of My privacy!"

An hour before, beside the shore of the circumambulating whirlpool, He had hit you with the rain of His reproach. Standing in the you of your youness, you were placed upon the feet of your individuality, beside the people. You were a spectator of the masses. He called you a valueless particle, putrid clay, dried mud, alluvial flood, like baked earth and a piece of potted clay. The flowing, moving flood has a destination which makes the hajj and does not stand still. It takes on no rottenness. It does not become putrefied but goes, pure, roaring and raging, pounding down. It finds a Way, rock breaker, barrier destroyer and, finally, a garden and habitation, the streams of Paradise in the desert. You who remain from the flood become sediment, become glued to the earth, turn into dried clay and become hard, rigid and cracked. *"He created the human being from dry clay like that of earthen vessels."* (55:14)

And you cover the earth, the farms, the flowers and plants. Thousands upon thousands of seeds where in every one the ardency and rapture of regeneration awaits impatiently for the splitting, opening and appearance from the soil to scatter leaves and fruit, to grow tall under the sky, under the sun, to open lips. You bury them under the earth. You make them rot. You make them die. You destroy them.

"While indeed fails he who pollutes it." (91:10)

The flood flows, intoxicated, clear, life-giving and with Christ-like breath.

And if you remain in a hole, isolated in monasticism, in individuality, in the pool of being as you be, isolated, silent and imprisoned, surrounded by your self's individuality, whether you receive pleasure or mortify yourself, you will rot and turn into a swamp. The worms of hundreds of diseases will nest in your heart. It will regenerate, will be reborn, will die in your soul and change the color of your skin. Your features will change. Your perfume will change. You will become the grave of a corpse, become a marsh. You will rot, become a swamp. *"Putrid clay."* (15:27)

O how good it is to emerge from a stone.
Moving head to head with the stones.
Moving smoothly if there is a plain.
Descending fast if there is a valley.
Your heart, however,
Is like a swamp—
Stagnant, motionless, calm and silent.

Flow. Become a flood.
Pound, sweep, wash
And arise.
Make the hajj!
Join the whirlpool of circumambulating masses. Circumambulate!

And now, an hour later, after circumambulation, when your head had descended into the sea of annihilation, into the lover masses, into the whirlpool of the circumambulaters of humanity, you drowned. You released mortal self—the self which faces itself for survival is in the masses who face towards God. You swarmed in the wave of non-existence. You rotated in the course of the masses upon God's circuit. Then you were placed in the orbit of eternity, in the orbit of the infinite sphere.

Now you have become Abraham!

THE STATION (*maqam*) OF ABRAHAM

Your Divinely created self, the Spirit of God which was within you, was in the swamp of the you-ness of you! Your head arises from the whirlpool. From where? From the same corner where you began under the Hand of God—the Right Hand of God. Now you have become self. You have attained your real me by annihilating all of your false me's. You are in the pure, white dress of *ihram* in the sanctuary of God, in the role of Abraham.

You stand in the Station of Abraham, step in the footprint of Abraham, stand facing God and recite your ritual prayer for Him.

You are Abraham, history's great idol-destroyer, the

founder of monotheism in the world, who carried the mission to guide the people upon his shoulders, the patient-rebellious, the rebel-guide, a Prophet—anguish in his soul, love in his heart, enlightened mind and—an axe in his hand.

The manifestation of faith arising from out of the heart of infidelity (*kufr*), the gusher of monotheism (*tawhid*) arising from out of the swamp of multitheism (*shirk*).

Abraham—the idol-destroyer of mankind's tribe—from the home of Azar—the idol-carver of his tribe!

The idol-destroyer, Nimrod-slayer, crusher of ignorance and tyranny—Abraham. The enemy of sleep. The rebel against the tranquility of humiliation and the security of oppression. The leader of the tribe. The pioneer of the Movement: life, motion, direction, idea, hope, faith and monotheism.

You are Abraham! Step into the midst of the fire—the fire of tyranny, ignorance—in order to save humanity from the fire—the fire of tyranny, ignorance.

The fire which is part of the destiny of each responsible human being, responsible for illumination and salvation.

But the God of monotheism turns the fire of Nimrodians into a red rose for the Abrahamians!

You will not be burned. You will not turn into ashes. The purpose was that you move through *jihad* by going towards—the fire—so that the self is offered in moving to save the masses from the fire, until the most painful of martyrdoms.

You are Abraham! Sacrifice your Ishmael with your own two hands. Place your knife at his throat in order to remove the knife from the throat of the masses, the masses who have continuously been slaughtered at the feet of palaces of power built from plundered treasures and at the threshold of deceiving, humiliating temples. Place the blade against the throat of your own Ishmael so that you gain the power to take the blade away from the executioner.

But the God of Abraham Himself pays the ransom for all Ishmaels.

You do not kill. You do not lose your Ishmael. The purpose is to move in the Way of Faith to the point where you have sacrificed your Ishmael with both hands, until the most painful of martyrdoms.

And now, O you who have come from the circumambulation of love, you are standing at the Station of Abraham. You have reached the Station of Abraham!

And when Abraham had reached here, he had passed the many phases of his eventful life from the breaking of idols, the destroying of Nimrod, the bearing of torture, the suffering of the fire, the struggling against Iblis, the sacrificing of Ishmael and—migrations, wanderings, lonelinesses, tortures and passing from prophethood to imamate. *"Behold, I make you an Imam for the people."* (2:124)

From individuality to the congregation, from being the son of the house of Azar, the idol-carver, to becoming the founder of the House of Monotheism!

And now he stands here, the snow of age upon his head, at the end of a life which resembles a history, appointed to build the House, to install the Black Stone, the Hand of God in the House of God and his partner—

Ishmael—who carries stones and hands them to his father. While standing upon this stone, his father lays the foundation of the House and builds it!

O wonder! Ishmael and Abraham are building the Ka'bah. Ishmael and Abraham—one passed through the fire and the other, the altar of sacrifice. Now, both are agents of God, responsible for the masses, architects of the most ancient temple of monotheism upon the earth, the first House of the People in history, the House of the Free, liberty, the Ka'bah of love, worship, a sanctuary, a mystery among the mysteries of the tent of cover, chastity and the angelic world.

And now you are standing in the Station of Abraham, stepping in the footprints of Abraham, upon the last step of the ladder of Abraham's descent, at the highest peak of Abraham's *miraj*, in the closest distance of Abraham to nearness.

The Station of Abraham!

And you, the founder of the Ka'bah, the architect of the House of Freedom the founder of monotheism, responsible, lover, aware, idol-destroyer, leader of the tribes, opposed to Nimrod's oppression, in combat against the ignorance of multitheism, in *jihad* against the temptations of Iblis, the satan (*khanas*) who places temptation in the breasts of the people.

Bearing homelessness, anguish, danger, fire and the slaughter of your Ishmael, and, now, no longer a House for your 'self' or a base for your 'Ishmael' but a House for the People, a shelter for the shelterless, a place secure for those pursued, the fugitives, the injured, the hunted who, bloodied and in fear, wander the earth, frightened and wounded, who find no shelter for everywhere

Nimrod is in pursuit.

A torch in this dark and longest night of the winter solstice. A cry on this night of tyranny.

A sanctuary, secure, clean and free for humanity, for the Family of God—the people—because everywhere disgrace and insecurity rule. They have made the earth into a grand house of prostitution, a place of murder, where every deed is forbidden except aggression and discrimination. O you who appear in Abraham's role, who stand in Abraham's Station, who stand upon the footsteps of Abraham and who give the hand of allegiance to the Hand of Abraham's God:

Live like Abraham and in your own age, be the architect of the Ka'bah of faith. Move your people out from the stagnant swamp of life, from the dead-like living, from the quiet sleep of the abasement of tyranny and from the darkness of ignorance. Give them direction. Call them to the hajj. Circumambulate.

And you, O ally of God! O in step with Abraham! O you who have come from the circumambulation, from the annihilation of 'self' in the circumambulating masses! You who have emerged in the shape of Abraham, who are standing in the place of the architect of the Ka'bah, founder of the sacred city, the Masjid al-Haram, and face to face with your ally —God!:

Make your land a sacred area
For you are in the sacred area.
Make your age a sacred time
For you are in the sacred time.
Make the earth into a sacred mosque
For you are in the Masjid al-Haram.
For 'the earth is God's mosque'

And you see that:
It is not.

THE SEARCH (sa'y)

You end your prayers of circumambulation in the Station of Abraham and resolve to go to Mas'a, located between two mountains—Safa and Marwah—a distance of more than 300 meters. You traverse this distance between two mountains seven times. You descend from Safa, walk until you are opposite the Ka'bah. You run, then return to your normal motion. You walk the rest of the way until the foot of Marwah.

The endeavor, the search (sa'y) is a struggle, a searching movement having a purpose—hurrying and running.

While circumambulating you were in the role of Hagar and in the Station, as both Abraham and Ishmael. Now that you begin the searching movement, you again return to the role of Hagar!

Everything is one here, all forms, moulds, appearances, titles, characteristics, personalities, limits, boundaries, distances, symbols, colors and patterns have been erased, have vanished—humanity uncovered and uncovered humanity.

Faith and love, belief and deed and nothing more.

Here no word is mentioned about any person, not even Hagar, Abraham or Ishmael for these are merely words and ideas here, not individuals or persons. Whatever exists is movement and constancy, humanity and Divinity and, in the midst, only discipline.

The hajj is this, is making an attempt. It is a continuous movement towards a constant direction and the whole world is this.

And now, a search.

Here you are as Hagar.

A woman from a despised and lowly African race. A female slave. A black Ethiopian woman. The slave girl of a woman: Sarah.

All of these exist in mankind's systems, in a system of *shirk*. But in the system of *tawhid*, this slave woman is addressed by God, is the mother of great Prophets of God, Messengers of God and manifestation of the most magnificent and dearest of values which God creates.

She is the first heroine in the drama of the hajj, the most conspicuous figure and, in the sacred area of God, only the remains of a woman—a mother!

In accordance with the command of love, she left her habited town, house and her family, took her nursing baby and moved to these stern and rocky mountains, alone, without anything, without anyone.

Only with love.

She came as God had Commanded, laid her child on the bed of the valley, a dry, scorched, waterless valley, without plant—nothing. The valley of fear, loneliness, death!

Absolute trust.

O wonder! God so Commanded. God said, "I will guarantee you your child, your life, your future and your needs. O Hagar! Manifestation of submission and obedience! Great heroine of the faith of love, of the trust of love, you are under My care."

Hagar, in submission and obedience, laid down her child in the middle of the valley as God Commanded and love so desired.

Then, Hagar, the heroine of submission and content-ment, hurriedly arose alone and began running in the dry and burned out mountains surrounding Makkah in search of water. Overwhelmed with the effort, move-ment, endeavor, aspiration, determination and self-re-liance, upon her own feet, with her will-power, her thought. A woman, a lonely mother. A migrant, respon-sible, struggling, searching, lover, faithful, bewildered, anguished. Without support. Without shelter. Without a society. Without a class. Without a family or a race. Homeless. Without hope, yet hopeful. A captive, a stranger, a slave woman, without family. Exiled by hatred. Rejected by the aristocratic system. Abased by people, race, class and even rejected by her family. A black slave woman with a child at her bosom, rejected from her home, town, country of the superior race. A wanderer in a strange desert. The prisoner of remote mountains and, now, alone and diligently, tirelessly determined, unfamiliar with despair, full of struggle, a migrant in the midst of the mountains.

Alone.

Running over the high peaks of soundless moun-tains in search of water. The Prometheus of the culture of Abraham—not a god but a slave woman. Not the seeker of fire, but of water.

Water? Yes. Water. Not a mysterious thing. Nothing supernatural. Not love. Not submission. Neither sur-render nor servitude nor the water of life—no.

The water of the spirit? Spiritual water? Illumina-tion? Heaven? No. No. No.

Drinking water!

Not what rains from the throne but that which gushes up from the earth.

[Material materiality.] The same liquid which flows over the ground and material life thirsts for. The body is in need of it. It transforms into blood in the body. It transforms into milk in the mother's breast. It is liquid in the mouth of a child.

Struggle in the search for water, a manifestation of the material life, the earthly life. An objective need. The link between humanity and the soil of the earth. The paradise of this earth. An earthly table.

A search. A material work. A material struggle. Struggling and working for water, for bread, to quench your thirst, to satisfy the hunger of your child, to live well. A thirst is awaiting and you are responsible in this scorched desert to find a spring, water, a gift, yea.

A searching movement. A struggle with the soil over the earth in order to secure your needs from the bosom of nature and take water from the depths of stones.

A search, absolute material, need—material deed—material goal—material.

Economy, nature, struggle!

It means need, material, human being.

Absolute intellectuality!

O wonder! It is only a few steps from the circumambulation to the search. A few moments and yet so much distance between.

The distance between two opposites—two contradictions:

Circumambulation: absolute love.

Search: absolute intellect.

Circumambulation: all Him.

Search: all you.

Circumambulation: Divine predetermination and that is all.

Search: humanity's free will and that is all.

Circumambulation: a butterfly rotates around a candle and keeps on rotating round and round until it burns, turns into ashes and goes with the wind. It becomes nothing. It vanishes in love. It dies in light and is negated.

And search: an eagle flies over the peaks of hard and black mountains with the long wings of its will-power in search of food. It snatches its bait from the heart of rocks. Heaven and earth are within its range. Winds are the tamed of its flight. Far horizons limit its sight. All space is a manifestation of its will-power. The expanse of the earth is under its wings. The hard, rocky mountains of the earth are weakened and submit to its two sharp, proud eyes.

Circumambulation is a human being enamored of the Truth.

Search is mankind, the self-developed of reality.

Circumambulation is the exalted human being.

Search is the powerful human being.

Circumambulation is love, worship, spirit, beauty, sacrifice, martyrdom, ethics, goodness, value, spirituality, subjectivity, truth, faith, piety, mortification, humility, servitude, gnosticism, illumination, the heart, submission, Divine Will, meta, heaven, unseen, predetermination, obedience, reliance, others, people, religion, the Hereafter, Resurrection and God—everything which inflames the Eastern spirit.

And search: intellect, logic, need, life, reality, objectivity, earth, material, nature, prosperity, thought, science, industry, policy, profit, pleasure, civilization, economy, instinct, body, free-will, choice, domination, world, power, livelihood and self—everything which causes Western endeavor.

Circumambulation is God and nothing else.

Search is humanity and nothing more.

Circumambulation is the spirit and nothing else.

Search is the flesh and nothing more.

Circumambulation is the pain of existence, the anxiety of heaven.

Search is the pleasure of living, the tranquility of the earth.

The circumambulation is to seek thirst.

The search is to seek water.

The circumambulation is as the butterfly.

The search is as the eagle.

And the hajj is the combination of opposites, the solution to the oppositions that have preoccupied humanity throughout history—material vs. ideal, intellect vs. illumination, this world or the next, pleasure or piety, free-will or decree and, finally, reliance upon God or the self.

The God of Abraham teaches you both. A lesson given not with philosophy, gnosis, science or words but with an example, a human being.

This great lesson of God should be sought and studied by philosophers, gnostics and seekers of faith and truth in the countenance of this human being—a woman, a black Ethiopian woman, a female slave.

Hagar. A mother.

She submits herself absolutely to Him in accordance

with love. She brings her child from the town, country, living place to this scorched, waterless, uninhabited valley. She lays him on its bed.

Disregarding all accountings and reckonings, with absolute trust, solely with the power of faith, with reliance on love and Him and nothing else.

Circumambulating.

But she does not sit beside the child as a pious person awaiting a miracle. She does not wait for a hand to descend from the unseen world to do something or for a table to descend from heaven or for a brook to flow from Paradise or just trust to meet her needs.

She leaves the child to love and immediately begins searching. She runs upon her self-determined feet and seeks with her able hands.

And now, amidst the dry, uninhabited mountains around Makkah, a human being, alone, thirsty, responsible, a stranger, a migrant in a fruitless search for water!

O joy! Are the words about Hagar or about a human being?

But her search ends in failure. She returns to her child in despair.

She sees, O joy! The child, left to love, being impatient in his thirst, has dug out the sandy ground with his feet. At the end of despair, in the final futile effort, in the moment no one could foresee, nobody could expect, suddenly , miraculously.

With the power of need and the mercy of kindness.

A humming.

The sound of the footsteps of water.

Zamzam.

The overflowing, sweet, life-giving water from the

depth of stone!

And the lesson!

Finding water through love and not through search but only after searching.

Reaching Him—not with just effort—O you who trust in love—endeavor as much as you can! Struggle! O you who have relied on love! O you who have absolute faith, absolute trust!

Seven times—exactly as in the circumambulation!

But not in a circle, for a circling effort is as an ass's milling effort, a futile rotation where, at the end, you reach the beginning, a hollow circle. That is, futility, absurdity, without content, without aim, like a zero. Working to eat, eating to work and finally death.

No. Rather, living not for the sake of living but for God. Searching not for the sake of searching but for people. Movement on a straight line and not a rambling one. A way and migration from a beginning to an end and from a point to a destination, from a start to an extreme, from Safa to Marwah. Going and coming seven times. Repetition in odd numbers, not even. Your search will not end in Safa where you would arrive at where you began.

Seven times. It means perpetually, tirelessly, all your life. Reaching towards Marwah is beginning from Safa— sensing pure love towards others—and ending in Marwah—the end of humanness. That is, attaining goodliness (*murawat*) and passing with magnanimity over the abnormalities and defects of others.

Which others? Your fellow companions in your search?

How I do not know.

What I know is this:
Raise your head in love from the whirlpool of self-non-existence. Place your footprints upon those of Abraham and then, Hagar-like, O human being, lonely stranger, wanderer, exiled in the desert of the earth! O human being, responsible, thirsty and searcher for water in the mirage of life.

Ascend the hill of Safa. Observe the white stream of wandering, struggling human beings. How restlessly and in thirst do they descend from the heights of Safa. Hurry in search of water over the burned gravel of this desert. Flow towards Marwah. Ascend the high mountain of Marwah and find no water. Return with empty hands, eyes full of anxiety, lips burning with thirst and again arrive at the dry rock of Safa. See that you have arrived at the same place from where you began. You hastily go and again arrive in Marwah where you had been and return to Safa where you had been and hastily go again. Seven times. Till eternity.

Finally, you find no water but reach Marwah.

And you, a drop, throw yourself from the heights of Safa into this white, wandering, struggling, thirst-quenching stream! Drown yourself in them. Descend and search along with others. At the halfway point, opposite the Ka'bah, run in the harmony of others.

THE END OF THE SHORTER HAJJ

At the end of the seventh endeavor or search upon the heights of Marwah, remove your *ihram*. Cut a piece of hair and put on the clothes of life. Free yourself and depart from Mas'a at Marwah. Go towards your Ishmael, alone, thirsty.

Listen! Do you not hear the humming of water in the distance?

Look! Thirsty birds are flying over this rocky place.

Zamzam has quenched Ishmael's thirst and a tribe from the most remote of places has filled the solitude of this valley.

The thirsty of the earth have come from the far horizons of the desert. They have erected tents around your Zamzam. A town grows from stone. A rain descends from revelation in this dry valley of despair. A house is born from revelation and love. And you, O returned from the search, so thirsty and so lonely.

Your loneliness has ended. Zamzam flourishes at the feet of Ishmael. People have encircled you. And what do you see? God has made a House, wall to your wall. Your skirt has become God's. O exhausted by the search! Lean on love.

O responsible human being! Endeavor, for your Ishmael is thirsty.

O you loving human being! Desire! Love will give you a miracle.

And for you, O pilgrim, who have returned from the search, from the thirsty desert of your being, from the depth of your solidified nature, a spring has opened.

Place your ear by the side of your heart. Press gently. You will hear it humming.

Go towards Zamzam from the rock mountain of Marwah. Drink from it. Wash yourself in it. Take from it. And take some to your land and offer it to your people.

PART TWO:

THE LONGER HAJJ
(tamattu')

Hajj is a ritual in two phases. That which has passed was the *umrah*, the shorter hajj. After passing through it you are free of the *ihram* and that which the *ihram* had forbidden until the 9th of Dhihajjah when the second phase begins.

It is the 9th day of Dhihajjah. Now the hajj begins, the longer hajj. Where are you? Whether you are in the Masjid al-Haram, beside the Ka'bah, alley, street, bazaar, hotel. It is not important. The resolve is release. It is the beginning of a great journey. Put on your *ihram* and leave Makkah!

O wonder! Now you must leave the Ka'bah. Leave Makkah behind.

By the way, where is the *qiblah*?

It is the hajj and by leaving the Ka'bah, it begins!

Then what was your resolve from wherever you are towards the Ka'bah? What was taking off and arising to go to the Ka'bah? What was the journey which included the Ka'bah? The shorter hajj, *umrah*!

And now the journey which is beginning? What is the journey from the Ka'bah, leaving Makkah? The longer hajj (*tamattu*)!

To intend the Ka'bah is not the hajj. The goal of the hajj is not the Ka'bah. You had thought so at the beginning. This is erroneous. Now learn that the hajj is not going to the Ka'bah. It is to depart from the Ka'bah. Now, experience it with your soul. Learn from the monotheism of Abraham that:

From the very beginning, the destination was not the Ka'bah. Everything begins from beyond the Ka'bah. You attain the end of the boundary of self at the Ka'bah. O migrant who has resolved upon Him! You will enter another land from the Ka'bah. You will take another way. The question is no longer about leaving the self and leaving your house. You left these things in *miqat*. Now you are leaving the House of God.

Now you who are in the highest heights, at the peak of servitude, have attained freedom and in the perfection of selflessness, you attain 'self'; you have gained the worthiness to be told: "Leave the Ka'bah."

You yourself now are closer than the Ka'bah. The pilgrimage to the Ka'bah has ended. The Ka'bah has brought you out from you-ness to selflessness. You go until God! No longer make the hajj to the house but make the hajj to the Lord of the House.

Here the question relates to orientation, not destination. The point is the direction of the Ka'bah, not the Ka'bah.

Wherever you stop, you will remain. You will die! O haj! Resolver. Departer. O perpetually moving towards

Him. O perpetually becoming unto Him. O human being, Spirit of God. O deed! A righteous deed. Have you come to Makkah? Do not even stop in the Ka'bah, nor stay in the sacred area.

The Ka'bah is the *qiblah* until you reach it so that you do not lose orientation or be deceived by other *qiblah*s. In the Ka'bah, the orientation is elsewhere. Resolve to go there. Resolve to undertake a great journey, greater than the journey to the Ka'bah: the longer hajj!

This is why on this day of departure, wherever you are, put on your *ihram* and leave Makkah! The longer hajj is to leave the *qiblah* behind.

What place is more honorable than the Ka'bah? You go until you find it.

ARAFAH (*knowledge*)

You put on the *ihram* and leave Makkah for the East. Upon your return from Arafah to the Ka'bah, you will stop in Mash'ar and then in Mina.

Why? Let's go and see. Go from the Ka'bah to where? To the farthermost point, the end of the Way.

Do not stop along the way! Phase by phase, gradually, move upon the way all wayfarers have gone. First, the first station. Second, the second station. Third, the third station. Rationally and logically.

This is the monotonous, often repeated lessons of teachers, spiritual guides and professional admonishers. These are subjects of compositions, traditional disciplines, arrangements and reconciliatory transactions. Throw all of these into the *ihram* of Makkah and escape in thirst and restlessness.

O you lover. You are in motion beyond the Ka'bah. One breath until eternity. Do not stay in the middle of the way!

Pause in Arafah on the 9th. Pause in Mash'ar on the night of the 10th. From the morning of the 10th until the 12th and, optionally, until the 13th, pause in Mina.

There is not a single sign to justify or explain the arrival and pause in the land of Arafah, Mash'ar and Mina. There is a straightaway of 25 kilometers between Arafah and Mina which connects the valleys of Makkah.

This uninterrupted line has no natural, historic or religious particularities. That which divides this way into three phases is an agreement, an assumed agreement for regulating the phases of the hajj.

That which makes the issue more sensitive is that here the emphasis is upon pausing. That is, your major duty in Arafah is pausing. Your main duty in Mash'ar is pausing. You have no basic task but pausing in Arafah or in Mash'ar. You collect seventy stones from the ground around you and only this. This cannot be the reason for pausing in Mash'ar and you must remain there from night to sunrise.

The emphasis in Mina is also upon pausing. On the day of the 10th (the Day of the Festival), the major tasks which end by noon are stoning and sacrificing but you must pause there for three days.

What does pausing mean? Pausing is hesitating. The passer of a passer-by in passing, not remaining, not residing, not staying but hesitating.

It means you are upon the Way in movement. Stop overnight in a place on a day and then move on. Also, you are only a wayfarer, a passenger, a pilgrim in these three residences. You have resolved upon a certain destination. Sometimes you stop with a caravan. When the signal to depart is given, the caravan decamps. You move with the caravan and leave the lodging for another.

It is an entrance, a pause and then a migration! The day in Arafah, night in Mash'ar and with the sunrise of the Festival (*eid*), in Mina. And in Mina, a three day pause!

But Mina is not the final stop nor the destination. Then when will the journey end? Where is the final destination of this caravan? Never. Nowhere. Then to what direction is it directed? Towards God.

Until when, until where? Where is the final residence? God is Absolute, Eternal.

Movement towards absolute beauty, absolute science, absolute power, absolute perfection. An eternal, restless, infinite movement. Towards God is the Way.

In this journey, God is not the lodging place but a direction. Everything changes, passes, is annihilated in us. Only direction is fixed. Only movement is infinite. *"All things perish except His Face."* (28:88)

We leave the Ka'bah and immediately go to Arafah and from Arafah, phase by phase, we return to the Ka'bah. *"We belong to God and unto God is the Return."* (2:156)

Everything relates to movement, an inherent movement, a transferred movement and everything is oriented to Him, not in Him!

This is why the hajj is absolute intention. This is why it is not a journey for a journey has an end. It is not a pilgrimage to a shrine for a devotee has a destination. It is hajj, absolute resolve, absolute purpose. Resolve exists but without a destination.

When you are in Mina, you are released and upon the return from Arafah, you do not reach the Ka'bah. You come close to the walls of Makkah.

There is proximity but no attainment! Therefore, the hajj is to go from the Ka'bah to Arafah and return from Arafah towards the Ka'bah until Mina.

In returning towards the Ka'bah, towards God, there are three phases—thus here we are not speaking about three lands—Arafah, Mash'ar and Mina are not three places. It is the secret of three phases. What led me to discover this secret was that I saw nothing in the land of these three stations.

Whatever exists, exists in the pauses of these three phases. We do not intend a deed but rather a pause!

Therefore, it is not really three places but three pauses! How can we come to know the meaning of these three phases? God Himself has named them. These Words descended from heaven.

Arafah comes from the word meaning knowledge. Mash'ar comes from the word meaning consciousness. And Mina comes from the word meaning love, faith.

From the Ka'bah, suddenly in Arafah,*"Surely we belong to God..."*

From Arafah towards the Ka'bah, stage by stage, upon the return, and *"unto God is the Return."* (2:156)

Therefore, knowledge (Arafah) is the beginning. It is the beginning of our birth in this world! It is the story of Adam, the birth of human beings and the creation of mankind on earth after the Fall—the beginning of the life of mankind upon the earth. It was here at Arafah (knowlege) that Adam and Eve came to re-know each other.

Arafah. The Fall? The exodus of Adam from the Garden of Paradise. This paradise is not the promised one. It is the garden of the earth, *jannah*. It is the earth covered with greens and trees. It is the birthplace of the first human being who, in that age when, far from responsibility and labor, ate, drank and enjoyed life, lived full and filled.

Until Iblis—the only one of God's angels who refused to fall prostrate before Adam, in whom God had inspired both evil and piety—began temptations. Iblis made him breach the limit, revolt against the prohibitions, eating the forbidden, namely, that which gives you a Divine quality: vision and immortality!

Adam first refused it. It means that there is something other than the intellect operative in human being. Iblis returned. Love. This time Adam and Eve ate the forbidden. All of a sudden, intellect and love shocked the angelic soul and turned him and her into the human being. The human being: this only angel who can commit sin and then repent, revolt, therefore, obey.

Revolt? It means a will which confronts the Will of God. It means freedom before the forces of nature. It means selection, then responsibility. It means consciousness of self. Consequently, the conversion of the garden of fullness, being filled and lacking anguish to the indigent earth, thirst and pain, the Fall.

The beginning of life of aware, responsible and rebellious creatures, eternally condemned to suffer anguish and thirst. Exiled. Feeling strangeness and captivity in nature. The free bird of heaven in the cage of earth. And, then, the inextinguishable anxiety of separation. The moaning reed flute upon the lips of religion, wisdom, gnosis, art and literature and ...life. In anguish from being cut from the reed-bed. The heavy and intolerable force of responsibility, anxiety for the rebellious soul. The instinctive anxiety of sin. The natural ardency for the return.

And now the hajj, the drama of creation, repentance: Consciousness of self and the feeling of being away from home. Exiled and, as a result, intending to return.

The conversion of the heavenly Adam and Eve to the earthly ones. The realization of human beings in its present concept. The rebellious human beings. The destroyers of barriers. A weakening before Iblis. Expelled from heaven. Being left to themselves by God. Exiled upon the earth. Prisoners of nature. All of these just for eating the forbidden which brought them rebellious wisdom, consciousness of self and a special insight unto God. It opened their eyes and they recognized their nakedness and himself and herself.

The Fall from the Ka'bah in knowledge (Arafah). The appearance of the birth of the human being on earth. The appearance of the human being at the time of the appearance of knowledge. The beginning of knowledge with the realization of one another and the first spark of love!

The encounter of Adam and Eve.

When Adam and Eve re-knew each other, their own kind and encountered the opposite sex who enjoyed the same nature as he or she, the human being, as an essence, with philosophical insight and its beginning— the appearance of knowledge.

And here, the human being with a cognitive perspective as an objective creature whose beginning in history—the appearance of knowledge. And in the hajj, the first move from knowledge (Arafah)! It is because of this that the pause in Arafah is during the day. It begins at noon of the 9th day when the sun is at its peak. The beginning of consciousness, vision, liberty from the captivity of nature, familiarization, link of affection, the knowledge of nature and the human being, under the clear light of the sun.

With the sun setting, the pause in Arafah (knowledge) ends. It is impossible to see in darkness. There is no possibility of familiarity or vision—no sight exists.

The sun sets in the plain of Arafah. The human being, accompanied by the sun, migrates towards the West. Movement at night. Pause in Mash'ar, the land of consciousness and consciousness of self. The phase after knowledge, consciousness.

And how surprising! First knowledge, then consciousness. Everyone thinks consciousness comes first in order to lead to knowledge and understanding. But the Creator of knowledge and consciousness says the opposite. From the encounter—the encounter of two opposites, the collision of two thoughts, conjunction and birth of the first collision and understanding, the end of individual living, the beginning of the first society, family, the appearance of the love of consciousness of self.

However, from the union of two beings appeared knowledge and with that, human beings on earth. Then the transformative course of knowledge led to consciousness. Cognition increased the power of understanding and consciousness gave birth to consciousness of the self!

The external world is the base for subjectivity. The intellect grows from the relationship of the mind in contact with the realities of the external world. Comprehension and perception gain strength and then the spiritual powers of a human being blossom.

If first there is consciousness (Mash'ar) then knowledge (Arafah), it is imaginary idealism.

If first there is love, faith (Mina), then it becomes gnosis, a way which lacks consciousness (Mash'ar) and knowledge (Arafah).

Knowledge (Arafah) without consciousness (Mash'ar) and love (Mina) is materialism. Scientism without God, without consciousness of self, cognition left over in phenomena—absurd life, spiritless civilization, ideal-less progress.

Consciousness (Mash'ar) and love (Mina), without knowledge (Arafah), is religion as everyone understands it. But in the religion of Islam, mankind is an earthly phenomenon of most inferior material yet in movement with the power of the Divine Trust which begins with knowledge. The understanding of the realities of the universe—materialistic view. And from that station it reaches human consciousness of self. This consciousness, the station between Arafah and Mina, is born of knowledge and gives birth to love and from that base, jumps over the highest peak of ascent, the final phase of perfection, ascension to heaven *"until the Lote-tree of the Boundary"* (53:14) until God! Love (Mina).

Realism! Yea. Not as a goal but as a principle. A base for the flight towards the ideal and beyond.

An idealism with a materialistic foundation. The human being in this school of thought is a contradiction, a combination of oppositions. Half—the earth, a bad smelling clay, sedimentary and petrified layer of a flood and within, the Spirit of God. And you? A deed, a freedom, a choice, a migrator from a muddy marsh to the Spirit of God.

In this journey you pass three phases, these places of pause: knowledge, consciousness and love (Arafah, Mash'ar and Mina).

And now we see so clearly and precisely how everything comes to light. Now simple and good. Religion? A way. Wisdom? Consciousness. The Divine Mission? Guidance. *Ummah*? A group in movement. Leadership? Showing the way. Leader? The teacher of the Way, guiding signs, martyr, witness, example. Worship? Smoothing and leveling the Way. Devotion and mortification of the soul? Revolutionary self-development of a responsible person to desert anything that invites you to itself, causes you to remain and weighs you down. The Way of God? A way that begins for God by deserting the self and sacrificing your world for the people. Prayer? The desire to call unto Him by expressing and offering our needs, requests, loves and disgusts to God having convinced the self and people. Remembrance? Reminding and forgetting not. The hajj? Resolving.

And even the solution to all oppositions and contradictions that we imagine? Wealth—good, a virtue, the Grace of God, the world and calamity, as well. That is, all things must be weighed and evaluated upon this Way. If the ritual prayer prevents one from going, then, *"woe to the praying ones."* (107:4) If money is used upon the Way, then the Prophet also liked the liking of money.

Now we have arrived in Arafah, the farthermost distance we will be from the Ka'bah on this journey. A dry plain, swelling from the soft sands of the seaside and located in the center, a small, rocky hill, the Mount of Rahman which the Prophet used as a pulpit on his last pilgrimage to give a message to the people.

An astonishing town, growing in a single day from the sands and dismantled at the time of evening ritual prayers. A complete town of nations without a government. A community of human races, colorless. A combination of all countries of the world, no frontiers. The whole earth upon a plain, the rows of white tents stretched from horizon to horizon. Discriminations! How few. Aristocracies showing themselves occasionally: How inferior. Aristocratic beauties: How ugly! And you ask what remains here that I have come for the pilgrimage? What action should I be performing? None. You are free. Float in the endless sea of humanity. Spend the day as you wish, even in sleep.

Let yourself feel you are in Arafah! Yet there is nothing to see here. As Andre Gide said, "Glory should be in the eyes of the beholder and not in what you look at."

There is no obligation here. That which you must do is greater than anything which can be shaped within the word 'obligation'.

Contemplation.

Take the bud of your primordial nature so it blooms under the clear sun of Arafah. And as to the habit nurtured by history, do not escape from the light and freedom.

O shadow nourished by oppression, secluded in ignorance, moss of the deep, calm swamps! O me! Leave your tent. Lose your 'self' in the depths of the ocean of people. Let the fiery sun of Arafah burn you.

Melt one day, O wax!

Luminous in the heart of the group yet not pliable in the hand of the enemy or a tame plaything in the hands of an actor! However, you are free this day to do as you like. Spend it in sleep like always. All that has been asked of you is to pause!

MASH'AR (*consciousness*)

The sun of Arafah leaves; so leave Arafah, as well, because knowledge also leaves. Knowledge cannot tolerate the night. The night swallows, kills and effaces it.

Do not spend the night in knowledge (Arafah).

Depart when the sun sets as people have resolved to depart. No Muslim can be found on the way to it when night falls. No. The city of the sun suddenly disappears in the ambiguity of the sunset as it abruptly escapes from the plain.

To where?

To consciousness (Mash'ar).

You are not free to rest; at every stopping place, a hesitation and immediate departure.

Stop? Never. Stay? Nowhere.

Pause. Half a day, a night and two or three days, that is all.

Tents erected yesterday are dismantled today.

They are talking to you.

With you. O ..'me'.

O you who are only a pause upon the earth and nothing more!

O you who are a short moment from the eternity of time and nothing more!

O nothing!

O wave! You whose comfort is your non-being. O who only exists in motion! O who becomes everything in resolving upon Absolute!

O...nothing.

O a drop.

Join the roaring stream of people! Flow!

"It is no fault in you that you should seek bounty from your Lord (in trade during the pilgrimage); but when you press on from Arafah, then remember God at the Sacred Waymark (Mash'ar al-Haram) and remember Him as he has guided you though formerly you were gone astray." (2:198)

Be in Mash'ar by nightfall, a valley stretching from Arafah towards Mina and Makkah. The closer it gets, the more narrow it becomes. People are more pressed into it.

Suddenly the storm of sunset agitates Arafah. It dismantles the one-day-town. The roaring flood of humanity—one color, one spirit, like a whirlpool around Mount Rahman, turn like a mill, a rotating whirlpool, anxious and worried from fear of the night. They pour down the narrow valleys and, like a roaring stream at night, the white flood of the masses leave the night, for night has occupied Arafah's valley.

And you are a point in this line of the Way. A drop like other drops. O you who flow! O Flood! O endeavor and roar at night! Faith and hope in darkness. Wonder!

Water reservoir

It seems as if the city of the sun melted under the me ᵤ.
Arafah. Now the city of sleep flows like lava on the
valley bed.

All have become lost in each other. Everyone is
drowned in the night and the multitude. But what is
there to fear? The road is safe and secure. The tragedy is
finding self and missing the way. But losing self upon
the way is salvation. Above all this, developing your self
as the way is worship.

Worship means: O rough, rocky place. O infected
marsh! O the highest peak of pride and the lowness of
abjection! Grind your self to become a smooth way
under the feet of God's Will so that it can flow over you
softly and gently and flow within you as in the essence
of life and the primordial nature of the world.

O you who God awaits at the end of the Way! Now
we have arrived in Mash'ar, the name of a place, the
place of consciousness! Observe the vigilance.

In Arafah knowledge was collective. In Mash'ar,
consciousness is singular, This means that realities are
varied and great in number but the truth is one and its
way, one! The way of people who move towards God!

And the Prophet, seated upon the earth, amongst his
Companions, traced several lines with his staff upon the
ground. He was unrestrained because knowledge is
found in understanding reality. It is a knowledge of that
which is. Knowledge (Arafah) is a mirror which reflects
patterns, colors, designs and conditions as they are.
Knowledge is a mirror before the world. Its name:
science.

That is all.

It has no good or bad. To serve or commit treason are

not pertinent to it. Ritual purity or impurity has no meaning in it. It is a science and only a science. It is one everywhere and always. *Kafir* or Muslim, the people or the enemy, traitor or servant.

These limitations appear with consciousness. A power which employs science, gives direction, creates debauchery or piety, war or peace, cruelty or justice.

In a capitalistic system, knowledge is the same as that of an equitable system. A Nazi physicist recognizes nature the same way as the Nazi's physicist victims do. The ulama of the Caliph know religion in the same way as the ulama who are captive of the Caliph.

What makes one an executioner and another a martyr? One a freedom seeker and the other a tyrant? One ritually pure and the other ritually impure? It is not knowledge and science. It is consciousness.

Which science? It makes no difference as science is one. Which kind of knowledge? The question is useless as knowledge takes only one form. But which consciousness? This question must be answered and the hajj answers it!

Sacred consciousness. That which is preserved in an environment of chastity, piety and purity.

It is because of this that the first phase was only knowledge (Arafah). Here it is not only consciousness (Mash'ar), but sacred consciousness (Mash'ar al-Haram).

How strange it is that the pause in sacred consciousness takes place at night and pause in knowledge (Arafah) during the day. Why?

Knowledge (Arafah) is a phase of science, the recognition of an objective relationship, an inner connection to an outer reality which requires sight and light but sacred consciousness is a phase of consciousness of self which contains the power of understanding and this is a subjective thing. The former is the sensation phase and objective witnessing: *nazar*. Here is the phase of thinking, inner consciousness: *basirat*.

Not irresponsible, polluted and sick thought or reckless consciousness but a responsible consciousness, committed to an environment of purity and virtue. In the sacred area of holiness and security of faith, sacred consciousness (Mash'ar al-Haram), like the sacred mosque (Masjid al-Haram), the sacred month (Dhihajjah), the sacred area (Makkah) where sin and corruption are forbidden along with aggression, fighting or harming living creatures or uprooting plants. Earth and time are sacred, secure, reverent and chaste. Within a barrier of piety, devoted to peace and goodness—pure, having been purified by the Spirit—luminous with the light of primordial nature!

O wonder. A consciousness born from knowledge gives birth to love and is a close neighbor, wall to wall, with science and faith, between knowledge (Arafah) and love (Mina) and after knowledge (Arafah) and before love (Mina).

It is because of this that sacred consciousness itself is luminous. It is an illuminated flame, lit by the oil of thought which lights the lantern of the heart.

Wisdom is consciousness of 'self' brought by the Prophets and bestowed upon humanity. It is this and not philosophy or science. It is that very knowledge which Islam speaks about. It is a knowledge which does not produce scholars but rather thinkers—with consciousness of self. It is not a subjective view of phenomena or methods. It is light and illumination. A light not outer but inner.

This is that knowledge which the Prophets of humanity called "the light which God places in the hearts of those He wishes." Knowledge of the Way. Knowledge of guidance. Everyone can learn knowledge but it is the knowledge of consciousness that is a light which God projects in the heart of anyone whom He desires.

Whom He desires? One who endeavors and struggles for God and not for self. "*As for those who strive in Us, We surely guide them to Our Path.*" (29:69). Knowledge of the Way. Guidance. A saving consciousness of self. The light of salvation. A special consciousness whereby a person from among the people (*ummi*) becomes the leader, the torch-bearer of the Way. The knowledge requires no literacy. It is not found in a classroom, book or notebook. It is not taught in religious centers or universities. Its center of learning is *jihad*. Its students are the *mujahid* from among the people who are the seekers of the Way to God.

This knowledge needs not a lamp nor the smoke of a lamp. It is itself the essence of illumination. Light. With it one can see, clearly see, even if it be night but the night of consciousness, sacred consciousness!

What matter that it is night and darkened space? Are you not upon the Way? Are you not amidst the multitude? With the caravan? A flowing drop in the midst of the white stream of people where the command is: "*Then press on from where the people press on and pray for God's Forgiveness.*" (2:199)

Gush forth and flow from where the people gush and flow. Flow into the groups of people, drowned among the people! What wonder! Seek out arms at night in the land of consciousness. For if it were not night what should one gather arms for? Why await the morning? And why the *jihad* of tomorrow? Consciousness. Mash'ar.

A pause to deliberate, plan, prepare the spirit, gather the arms. Mobilization in a land which borders the battlefield at a time which joins with the day of battle.

And all of this is the pious dissimulation of night, in hidden ambush, on the border of Mina during an oppressive rule! The gathering of arms in the darkness of night but in the light of sacred consciousness. Sacred consciousness with the acquired recognition in the light of knowledge. A night in anticipation, in anticipation of morning. A morning of light. A victory and love in Mina.

*****

The army, roaring and dishevelled, reaches Mash'ar. It hurriedly collects the stones upon the way from among the rocky mountains and then...tranquility, contemplation.

In this desert Gathering Place for the Day of Judgment, Resurrection, *mash'ar*. No. O God. *Sacred Consciousness*. There are no tents, signs, walls, doors, ceilings, street lamps or ramparts. Do not attempt to recognize anyone or find your caravan. It is useless. Everyone is alone in Mash'ar, that is all. Two. Everyone with the night incredibly filled with people. Crowds as flocks jammed together. Incredible.

The Gathering! *"The day on which a human being shall fly from his brother and his mother and his father and his spouse and his son."* (80:35)

Now, from non-self you have attained self and in negating self, proved it. You tore off the self in your own *miqat* with the *ihram*. You joined the multitude. You left your 'self' in the whirlpool of the circumambulation. You discovered self in the endeavor of searching. You gave your 'self' to the flood in Arafah (knowledge) and now take it back in Mash'ar (consciousness).

Everyone is alone in this huge crowd. O you who achieve 'self', become 'self'! That 'self' which is now truth, the non-false me.

Without clothes, without form, no longer adornment nor color nor mere mask nor margins. You who have become a pure content from head to toe. O you who are unmasked! O you who are you! Retire with the Friend tonight.

Now admit to the 'self' which you negated. To free the 'self' is to admit to the selfhood of 'self' with unreservedness, with bluntness, with frankness. Can you imagine what ardency this is?

Now the time has arrived for you to destroy the barrier, tear the curtain, release the life-long prisoner in your covered dungeon for there is you and only you.

You joined the multitude alone! Now, amidst the crowd, you reach aloneness. How precious is the individuality which you discover in the multitude. A pearl you search out by diving deep into the ocean, shoulder to shoulder with people but alone. How glorious it is! Be with the people yet be not with them. paradox

Here is Muzdalifah, a pressurizer, a compacter. A narrow passage, its embrace tightened, it presses the army in its arms.

Millions of people scattered in a frontierless, limitless desert. Not everyone is in a place but, far from others, not in a town but facing wall, wall, wall. Everybody in the cage of a room, the barrier of a house without others, covered, silent, locked in 'self' but in a narrow passage, all pressed together, side by side. All have crept together.

With all of this—everyone—the self—alone with this sky, with this world. It appears that in the absolute sovereignty of the multitude, one becomes more alone. No one has anything to do with the other. Fear not. Night embraces you with modesty. No look calls you to that which you were and are. Free yourself in the night.

What am I saying? In Mash'ar, only the land is covered by night. The sky of Mash'ar is the royal court of God, this silent and moon-lit palm grove. Take the bloody and restless fist of your heart and place it under the shower of its unseen silence. Like the butterflies of ardency, set free your captive eyes in this green field. Sense the strangeness of this painless desert in which you are condemned to live in the depths of your primordial nature. Hear the voice of God in the mysterious silence, the painful moaning of that great prisoner of the earth, the rightful leader of humanity who, beside this despicable city of life and in the heart of this soundless, earthly desert, puts his head at the edge of a well and cries.

The night of Mash'ar arrives with mysterious and magnificent glory and when faced by it, existence closes its lips and becomes tranquil.

Suddenly an invading flood hits itself against the valley of Mash'ar. Pressed and full of commotion, it

runs over the bed of the valley and gradually sits down
in the narrow embrace of Mash'ar, upon the skirts of
the surrounding hills and mountains. Then Mash'ar
becomes silent again under its endless ceiling.

The night of Mash'ar has begun. In Mash'ar, there is
no lamp. Night is illuminated with moonlight and with
the large, shining rain drops of stars, the lamps of
heaven!

The night of Mash'ar. This beautiful, heavenly creature, unrecognized by those who search for a loaf in the
earth. City and life-alienated people who have spent all
of their lives with their heads thrust into the earth. That
which they recognize is another night. The night of
Mash'ar is indescribable.

The night of Mash'ar is a shadow of the imagina-
tion-nurturing, heart-warming nights of paradise. Its
moonlight is cold, open and affectionate. It is the caressing smile of God and it is in its countenance that your
heart bears witness to the oath of God to moon and
moonlight.

The moonlight of towns with heavy smoke. Habita-
tions mixed with heavy dust. The steam of breaths
which are damp, dirty, dusty. The stars, yellow and
sick.

It is the night before the 10th of Dhihajjah and the
great army of monotheism—these worshipping *mujahids*,
armed gnostics—have become silent in this mountainous camp, drowned in their loving longings. They have
drifted into the observations of the sky of Mash'ar. They
are occupied with observing and drowned in this sus-
pended, green sea over which diamond-winged birds
of the stars appear one by one from the unseen upon the

ceiling of the black night of the earth, opening holes towards another world.

The moon with its glittering light which is the only caressing smile that nature shines on the countenances of the wretched of the earth, pours light from the top of the mountain into the valley of Mash'ar. Diamond flowers bloom. The invisible hand of an angel brings the beautiful lantern of the pleiades from a corner of the sky and hangs it upon the ceiling of Mash'ar. Then appears the clear and mysterious road as if it links directly to eternity, the Milky Way of Ali and the road to Makkah.

What does this mean? It is the road that Ali takes to Makkah. The multiple meanings interpreted by the masses at which scholars—those who stay in knowledge—laugh at for these truths are covered by myths which are more profound and more precious than history and their only crime is not to have found reality. And historians? They only understand events as virtues because they happened or have left traces. They do not realize what truths they have abandoned for they are amused with absurd superstitions, dirty abominations and detested lies. They waste their life and their knowledge. This is why it is said Prometheus is a figment of the imagination and Ayaz, the bearded and moustached lover of Sultan Mahmud, is real.

Look at the sky of Mash'ar.

Whenever despicable satans try to deceive by hiding oppression, tearing apart a bit of the night and visiting the pure sanctuary of heaven, the arrows of the guardian angels of the heavenly world of God, who are the holders of the curtain and keepers of the veiled sacred sanctuary of the heavens, shoot them down with meteorites as arrows of light which occasionally sink into the black life of night, driving them towards the desert of the earth so that the secret of His great chastity may not fall into the skulls of these despicable minds and they not hear and not understand with their deceit because the exalted sacred region should be spoiled by no satanic steps in the sacredness of the beauty and splendor of solitude and no forbidden person should be shown the way.

And you, O side by side with the people! Lost in the multitude even though in solitude of 'self' with God. O you who are an armed gnostic! O devotee of the night of Mash'ar tonight and lion of the day of Mina tomorrow! What do you carry with your self tonight in this army which awaits the morning of *jihad*? Have you erected a camp in the station of consciousness? Do you wear the dress of death with arms of war in hand and nothing else? Make your weapons the place of your refuge tonight. Keep them under your head in solitude with God. It is you and He, with your arms and your faith and nothing else in this pure and free aloneness. Ascend through the ceiling of creation for a few hours, through the opening of the stars of Mash'ar. Fly in the heavenly sphere. Set yourself free from the narrow enclosure of being and inferior world of living. O follower of Muhammad (ص)! Make the journey. Ascend to heaven. Kindle love in the crucible of your nature. Burn the weaknesses, fears, concerns and complexes which life has poured into you. Develop, cherish and prepare self for the morrow, tonight. O liberated servant! You who are a lover, a *mujahid*! You theist seeker of justice! Satan (the *khanas*) is awaiting in the battlefield of Mina; satans prevail over the land of faith. Prepare and ready self for the morrow, tonight. A horrible war will take place at dawn. Fill your hands tonight with bullets and consciousness of self in the station of consciousness and arms. Fill your heart with love through prayer.

You ask what relics exist here that we have come to visit as pilgrims and what action is to be taken here?

None. You are free. Float in this deep sea of humanity.

Spend the night as you like, even in sleep.

But feel you are in Mash'ar.

There is nothing to see here. Endeavor to keep the glory in your glance.

There is no duty here. That which exists is greater than the framework that duty could contain.

Contemplation.

Night spreads its tent over the hundreds of thousands of nameless and signless human beings upon the earth. Observe the sky covered with tiny stars.

Place your thirst under the sky of Mash'ar. Let the mysterious rains of inspiration quench it. The silence of Mash'ar overwhelms in this tumultuous resurrection. You clearly hear the voice of silence.

Nothing exists in this space to narrow the place of God in your mind. The space is overflowing with God.

You smell His Essence as clearly and simply as the aroma of a flower.

You see His presence with your eyes and hear in the depth of your soul like a caress, like love.

Mash'ar has the countenance of Islam. It is similar to Ali: A heart swollen with waves of love and a hand upon the sword. Everybody trains to be a Muslim in Mash'ar.

Devotee of the night, lion of the day.

Take the night of Mash'ar to dawn in the deliberation and the search for self.

Fly in the heavens of Mash'ar. Ascend with the spirit in your search for God.

Search the ground of Mash'ar in mobilization of *jihad*, in search of arms. It is an astonishing sight.

The roaring flood of migrants who arrive from Arafah abruptly scatter upon the hillsides like an army. They hurriedly disembark from their vehicles while still moving and hastily climb the mountains in search of arms.

It is the army of monotheism. Hierarchy plays no role. It exists but not in relation to individuals so much as in relation to the individual and God. There is no rank. There is and yet not one based upon name and title but upon primordial nature, in self and in relation to self. Today's self, your tomorrow's self and the self of your every moment.

It is the army of monotheism.

Abraham issues the commands!

Struggle to gather arms at night. Everyone is responsible for self, yet accompanying each other.

The next station is Mina. It is the place of combat. The day after is the day of sacrifice and time for combat. The war begins tomorrow. Thus everyone must be armed tonight. Combat takes place in the light of day but arms are collected during the darkness of night.

It is an astonishing scene. It is a great night. Greater than great. Time understands not such a night. But no. It understands it well.

The stormy and tumultuous sea of people think of combat and gather arms. Hundreds of thousands of mysterious spirits, all brothers, sisters, fellow thinkers, fellow warriors, everybody knows the other well. Nobody, neither brother nor sister nor husband nor wife nor mother or father nor friend or enemy see or recognize each other. Everybody thinks about his own deed in the darkness of Mash'ar; stoops down upon the earth; reaches among the stones; fingers and feels the stones searching for pebbles to throw in Mina.

What kind of pebbles? Pebbles, but not just any kind of pebbles. Be careful. It is dark and they are difficult to find. But they must be found. They must rightly be found, looked for, and precisely searched out. Each should be evaluated. Each has criteria, order. Everyone should execute accurate orders, discipline, unity, order, harmony, obeying the command, responsibility.

The story is very serious.

The pebbles you collect are your arms. They are your arms to fight the enemy.

It has so been ordered and you know what kind of pebbles to collect.

Smooth, polished, round, smaller than a walnut and larger than a pistachio.

What does it mean? It means: bullet.

Everything is reckoned, precise and with foresight. The next day every soldier of Abraham's army must aim seventy bullets towards the sensitive parts of the enemy in Mina: Head and breast, brain and heart. Any bullet shot which misses does not count or which hits the stomach and foot and not a sensitive place does not count. Foresee that your aim might be bad. Select more pebbles. Cover up for your lack of skill by providing more power. At any rate, you should not run short in the battle scene. If you miss a single shot, you are not a soldier. You have not participated in the hajj.

Here the word is military discipline.

Do not forget you must pause three days in Mina: the 10th, 11th and 12th. The 1st day is the attack against the last idol: statue, with seven shots.

Just taking a shot does not count. Only those which hit the mark. These are military acts. Reality is the criterion and action? An external effect, an objective result.

Here is the land of action. There is no monastery here. It is a scene of battle.

Orders are precise, decisive, inevitable and are as clear as two times two is four.

It does not have patience for Sufic, philosophical, ascetic justifications and interpretations. It is not the work of prayer, recourse and intercession, complaining, supplication, vowing, religious bribery, deceitful deceits and tricks and jurisprudential, philosophical and reckless imaginings of Sufis. It is absolute obedience, action and effect. It must be carried out in the minutest of details. Obedience here is unquestioned. There is no alternative. Nothing can replace it. No one can forgive your shortcomings. No one can bring pardon for you.

Forget not that in this mountainous region, no one is an authority. If Abraham (ع) or Muhammad (ص) missed a shot or have shot one less, they are responsible and have not performed the hajj. If you err, you must pay the penalty. There is no other way. Deceivers of the Divine Law are all bare-headed here.

physical aspect of touch - throwing the pebbles

The first day, attack with seven shots.

On the second and third, three attacks per day and in every one afterwards, again seven. This is forty-nine to here.

On the fourth day, you are free. You can either stay or go from Mina. If you stay, you must fight like two days before. In Mina, there is no day of peace and rest from war. If that is so, your total shots become seventy.

After supplying yourself with arms and easing up on the duty of *jihad*, the military spirit ends. Talk of war, steel, bullets, discipline, roughness, dry military view and performance of questionable orders immediately gives way to spiritual gnosticism and there comes serenity, peace, sincerity of heart, loving deliberations and ascension of the spirit.

The roar of the lion suddenly deforms into a painful moan. The uproar of shots gives place to silent words which shine through the absorbed eyes of heaven. In the depth of the night, conversing with God.

It is an astonishing scene.

This is not a mechanical society. It is a revolutionary *ummah*. The knowledgeable, those who practice, the politicians, the devotees, the worldly, the religious and ...are artificial borders for artificial, defective people but the *ummah* is a revolutionary society, a society not based on a series of class hierarchies. It is a society upon the way, a moving caravan, with One God, one way, one qiblah and all form one tribe, children of one father and servants of One God. **Its intellectuals fight, its fighters worship and its worshippers think.**

And now, in this scene which displays this *ummah*, armed *mujahids* have taken on a state of gnostic worshippers just as before in Arafah they had the visage of awakened intellectuals.

The night of consciousness sees that Mash'ar, all at once, takes on the rage and roar of a frightening army which is striving for a great conspiracy in the refuge of the mysterious night, at the border of the frontier of tomorrow. Then it becomes like a calm and limpid sea which makes peace with the night under the radiation of the moonlight and the rain of stars. It becomes the place of descent of the angels of beauty and the Mercy of God. Drowned in ponderous wonder, it takes on such a peaceful silence in which the sounds of the drops of the tears of the beloved can be heard and other than the throbbing of the hearts of lovers—for each of whom there is a story—no sound disturbs the subtle, quiet of Mash'ar.

Mash'ar, a mountainous camp for the only army in the world in which every soldier is a commander. But instead of the thoughtless intoxication and the brawling of pride on the night of battle—a battle that right now calls the victory of tomorrow, the night of the Festival—instead of that, the whisperings of love; the rapture of humility; the silence of wonderment before the uneasiness of destiny and allurements; the ardency at the threshold of eternity; the anxious thirst of the heart to attain *ithar*, to give of that which you yourself need, through devotions under the rain of revelation and purification of the self and to nourish and feed the spirit with reward of one's merit in battle, to receive the high rank of martyrdom from the Hands of the Great Commander because lives are in His Hands.

O wonder!

Mash'ar!

Arms in hand and prayers on lips, awaiting the morning of battle.

Morning approaches.

The dawn's breeze raises a mysterious commotion in the area.

Suddenly, harmonious cries of the Call to Ritual Prayer open wings from every side, mingle in each other, widespread and freely opening the way as if they hit the shore of existence from every side and return to Mash'ar.

Hundreds of thousands of figures in the ambiguity of dawn, break and fold down in *ruku* and *sajdah*.

The breeze of the Call to Ritual Prayer melodiously creating waves, blows smoothly over the white sown field of monotheism—the glorious unity which no ceiling or roof can contain.

Now is the time for the morning ritual prayer, the everlasting ritual prayer.

And here, it is unique.

The Call to Ritual Prayer becomes silent and Mash'ar sleeps for an hour.

Night escapes from Arafah, descends from the heights of the mountains, passes over those asleep in Mash'ar, pours into the valley of Mina and flees— morning brightness in its pursuance.

MINA *(love, faith)*

The longest pause, the last pause, the final station! That is: wish, goal, ideal and *mina, maniyat, amani, tamana* (willingness, aspiration, trusteeship, imploring) love! The last phase after the phase of knowledge and consciousness.

What Dante imagined to be two phases: imitating the most sublime ascension of consciousness and gnosticism of the East, the philosophy of illumination: wisdom of Virgil and love of Beatrice in the Divine Comedy.

But in the hajj—this great drama of Divinity—there are three phases: knowledge, sacred consciousness and love.

Now it is the great beginning. The hajj nears its highest peak.

Today is the 10th of Dhihajjah. It is the day of the *eid* (Festival), the *eid* of Sacrifice.

Morning pours into the narrow valley of Mash'ar and brings Muslims to their feet with its invitation of light.

From the bed of the valley, from the base of the mountains, from the crevices, major and minor routes, large and small streams of the ranks of the *mujahid*s, little by little, flow, link together and create a great stream, the narrow valley, narrower, the stream, more compressed and stronger.

The pause in Mash'ar ends. It is again time to migrate, pull up the roots of the heart from this station and move towards another.

The white army of monotheism has started to move. It has spent the night collecting arms, talking to God, anticipating the morning of battle! The devotees of Mash'ar, now—the lions of Mina!

Their hearts overwhelmed with flames, overflowing with rage, their minds filled with ardency and saturated with love. *Firm of heart against the unbelievers ...compassionate among themselves."* (48:29) They have resolved on Mina.

The land of God and Iblis.

Mash'ar is beginning to move. It moves towards the West; the most beautiful station lies ahead: the morning's smile, the morning of the Festival is causing everyone to be restless.

The army arrives at the valley of Muhassar, a valley of hardships, containing difficult, narrow passages. The command to hasten! The army, which still carries with itself the serenity of night, the pause and inner deliberations, quickly becomes agile, moves forward and hastens towards Mina.

Suddenly the roaring and forward moving stream hits a great impenetrable obstacle.

It retreats and ultimately is halted. Not even one step can be taken forward. It is only at the end of the army that a weak movement can be seen.

What has happened?

What obstacle in this world has the power to suddenly halt such a roaring stream in its place?

What command can issue such an efficient and decisive halt?

Who issued the command to halt?

The sunrise!

It issues the command to attack.

The army has arrived at Mina's frontier.

The front of this long, undisciplined and shapeless rank which appeared from the compressed swarming of millions of free soldiers and volunteer warriors who take no orders from anyone in the world is cut, with one sharp blade, and all stand on an imaginary line in army discipline. No one from the roaring, disorderly army dares to step forward. An invisible wall separates Mash'ar from Mina. No power in the world can destroy this steel wall, not even Abraham, not even the Prophet of Islam because it is not an agreement. It is not a law. It is a Norm from among those which exists in nature. It has been founded by He Who Founded knowledge, Who Founded the rules of nature, Who Founded the system which rules over the universe and no change, no conversion can be found in His Norm.

The command of the sun, like the forces of gravity and the order of life and death!

Here it is only morning that rules. Its subtle finger-tips have the ability to suddenly remove the impen-etrable obstacle in the way of this aggressive flood; let morning rise! Like a shadow which is sucked by the laughter of the light, this unconquerable wall—which so nails this powerful flood in place—is effaced with a smile!

Behind this invisible wall, restlessly stands the armed aggressors on disciplinary lines, in anticipation of the sun's command.

The vanguard of its rise has driven the night from everywhere but still moments are left before it appears on the rooftop of the East.

No where in the world, in no phase of time, over no *ummah* in the world, does such a sovereignty rule like the morning.

Melancholy struck people who, restless for love and battle, stand behind the gates of Mina, all their body and eye, looking towards the way of the sun until it arises behind the gateway.

Millions of eyes and hearts await the command of light in an inflamed silence, some being so restless and in need, hear a command before it is issued.

Why?

It is a command. This army is all of the power of monotheism upon the earth, the sole army in the world, in history, that takes its command from the sun. The only *ummah* who have accepted the sovereignty of morning. An *ummah* who alone accept the sovereignty of morning.

Morning arises from Arafah and breathes behind the mountains. The red aurora has split the black tent of enveloping darkness up to its neck and has sprinkled the blood of martyrs of tyranny and the sacrifices of multitheism over the countenance of the *eid* of Sacrifice. The army of monotheism calls for vengeance at the threshold of an uprising against the bases of history's three rebels against God: *taghut*s. The moments are moments full of glory and excitement. The sun and its luminosity, the aurora and its red incisive blade, morning and the pulsations of its breath...have made everyone restless. This sacred sign of God comes today with hand and lap full of the Promise and a caress, hope and faith, the command for battle and the glad tidings of victory. It comes to issue the command of attack to the idol destroyers. Today, the greatest base of Iblis upon the earth is smashed. Today *shirk* (multitheism) is obliterated. Today, *tawhid* (monotheism) is manifested in its most glorious countenance of love and self-sacrifice.

Suddenly a flood of light pours into the passageway. The sun appears on the peak of the mountain and issues the order to pass through.

The clamor of joy, the stream of sun and flood of people, all three mingle in each other and descend to the valley of Mina.

This multitude, now, is not only a group of white doves of peace, but more than that, they are armed *mujahids* of war.

It is because of this that the reference is made to order, discipline and command because:

Night must be spent pausing in Mash'ar.

On the day of the 10th, arrive in Mina.

The frontier of morning is the frontier of Mina. The line of morning separates night from day.

It is because of this that the command to pass the frontier, the command to begin the attack on Mina is in the hands of the morning sun of the 10th of Dhihajjah.

Mina is in the West and Arafah, in the East. The army is standing facing Mina. The sun rises from behind, from the heights of Arafah and pours into the narrow valley of Mina. The sun also undertakes a hajj. It rises in Arafah, passes Mash'ar and enters Mina.

The army of *jihad* and love, the *mujahids* who have come from Arafah and who hesitated the night in Mashar and have collected faith and arms there, must stand at the frontier of Mina, at the doorway of a town which is both the place of martyrdom and scene of battle, waiting, prepared and alert for the command of sunrise.

The sound of the footsteps of the sun.

Why?

Build yourself in the night, collect arms.

In the refuge of the night, collect arms.

Do not enter Mina before sunrise

Because the night is the speciality of pausing in Mash'ar.

Do not stay in Mash'ar after sunrise

As the day is the speciality of pausing in Mina—

Begin at the moment of the sunrise.

This sun is the sun of the 10th of Dhihajjah,

The time of the attack of Mina has begun.

The command of the sun is the command of time.

Obey the determination of time.

Only await the command of the sun.

Only anticipate the rise.

Only the sun of the 10th.

Only the rise of the *eid*.

O wonder!

There is still some distance from Mina till the bases of the idols.

There is still some distance from the place of arrival in Mina until reaching the front.

Eid should be celebrated after the battle; after defeating Iblis; after victory; after stoning the idols.

And you, O brother, look at the nation of monotheism, observe the tradition of this nation.

Eid is not celebrated for the defeat of an enemy, nor for the victory of a friend but before the battle begins, before reaching the battle.

It means you have attained victory when you have made a decision.

It means when you have stepped onto the frontier of Mina, you are victorious.

And...what am I saying?

How difficult it is to understand this simple nation.

And how complicated is this simple *ummah*.

It means whenever its time comes, you are victorious, for the time of victory arrives. If —you had come from Arafah. If—you had spent the night in Mash'ar, in deliberation and preparation, bringing them to the morning of *eid*.

No. No.

I have not mentioned the most important of if's. If you have come in the season. If you were present in the *miqat*. If you put on the *ihram*;

And...what am I saying?

Who are you?

Who am I?

The individual is good for nothing.

The Quran speaks about people, not an individual.

How beautiful is His Word: *al-nas*.

It has no singular form.

The Hand of God is in the multitude.

Movement, perfection, the vice-gerency of God in nature and... victory has been written in the fate of people, the unchangeable Norm of God in the life of the multitude.

And the determined route of history is towards realizing the plan of God in the creation of humanity.

You and I? That which we can do is to discover this Norm and rightly select this destined route: the determinism of history; the Divine fate of time; the decisive destiny of the life of humanity; and finally, the defined justice spreading revolution of the world for it is the God of Abraham and the Creator of humanity Who says: *"My righteous servants will inherit the earth."* (21:105)

And His Promise is to whom? *"We desired to show favor unto those deprived and to make them leaders and to make them heirs."* (28:5)

Deprivation! That which metamorphosizes and effaces human beings, destroys and steals all human capabilities and all of the material and spiritual powers of a person. Deprivation! A word which includes all anti-human systems and all paralyzing factors of humanity: despotism, colonialism, enslavement, exploitation, brain washing and all that from here on that the enemies of mankind may invent.

Let them invent, but God not only proclaims His Will for the salvation of the condemned people and the freedom of the wretched of the earth but He gives assurance that the Divine fate of history will place the reins of leadership and the guide of human society into the hands of this class. It will make the abased, in all places and for all times, the heirs to all palaces of power, treasuries of wealth and cultural and religious capital.

Deprived upon the earth! What a coincidence! *The Wretched Upon the Earth*, a book by Fannon.

On the Day of Resurrection, human beings who determine their destiny are evaluated and divided into two groups by the agents of God: the group of the saved and those who are destined for the inferno. Upon the earth, as well, the determiners of destiny who, here, are the agents of Iblis—have divided people into two groups, those destined for heaven and those destined for the inferno. According to Sartre—in the introduction to this very book—of the two billion people upon the earth—in terms of colonialists—five hundred million are human beings and one billion five hundred thousand are natives, the condemned, accursed of the earth, residents of the third world inferno!

But the natural determinism of history or Divine determinism of history—it makes no difference—has guaranteed the victory of the wretched or the deprived—it makes no difference upon the earth. The Divine Will has determined the course of the caravan of humanity's *ummah*, children of the martyred Abel. History's determinism is the unchangeable course of God. *"Thou shalt find no change in the course of God."* (33.62) God gives both existence to creatures and direction. *"Surely His are the Creation and the Command."* (7:54) And you, a sign; your fate depends on you discovering the determined course. History has its own and humanity follows its determined course.

And you? Prisoner of four determinisms, the four great prisons: nature, history, society and self! You should discover history, the philosophy of the science of history, and consciously place yourself upon its route and in harmony with history's determinism. You will alter your determined route of history. Discover the determinism of your social environment and recognize society's rules, employ them and with a conscious revolution, you will achieve freedom from the prison of the system ruling over society.

Release from all three prisons with knowledge. But what about the fourth prison? The prison of 'self'. The prison of instincts? The prison you bear in your nature?

Knowledge is impotent in opening up this fourth prison for the other three existed outside of your 'self', whereas this fourth prison is within you. Within you, it is your being learned. A knowledge which must famil-

iarize you with 'you', discover 'you'; a power which
must predominate over you, cause you to revolt against
your 'self' and a powerful arm to convert and transform
you from your 'self'.

And here no longer the knowledge as we see it which
is itself the great jailer of the scientist, rather, wisdom!
Knowledge of primordial nature, consciousness of self,
the light emitted by Prophets in the hollows of the earth,
religion. A wisdom that reveals your inner prison to
you, discovers the sleeping jailers in the depths of your
being and a power which releases you from the prison
of your self. No longer the industry of science but the art
of love! If your life has also become your prison, love
breaks it—with martyrdom. If your Ishmael becomes
an obstacle for you, love will kill it with your own
hands—with that which is higher than martyrdom.

Freedom from the fourth prison with love.

The knowledge which grants you consciousness of
self and Divinely-inspired creativity so that you yourself destroy it as nature built it—and construct it as God
Willed.

As you are only a being, you must create your own
essence yourself—because the human being is created,
has fallen into this desert and is left to himself. You? An
existence without howness. A nothing who can become
everything. A doubt, a vacillation, a possibility, an absurdity who can become a human being. Chose being
human. Discover your primordial nature (religion). Place
yourself in its route, conscious of self. Free yourself
from the prison of the determined self, harmonizing
with the fate of human beings. You can make a choice
and recognize the determined route of history for his-

tory is the flow of the human being in the river bed of time. It is a determined flow, a becoming towards God. And you, O to be nothing! Be becoming! Recognize the human being. Chose to be a human being for this determined stream is flowing. It is a perpetual flow. The sovereignty of night in Mash'ar and the rule of three tyrannies in Mina cannot stop or deviate the victorious course of this determinism because this is a Norm of God. For never shall you find any change in the course of God. *"And never shall you find in the course of God any alteration."* (35:43)

Your destiny is a text which the hands of writers will write it for you if you are not aware of it. If you know it, you can write it yourself.

And you —O nothing, O who are conscious and free, if you come to the *miqat* in season and recognize and choose the course of your primordial nature —the line of the course of determinism of the human beings—then you can become a smooth way under the feet of God's Will, a way that leads from a swamp to the Spirit of God. For here the rule is what God has Willed.

It is the rule of the determinism of knowledge and, at the shore of this flowing stream, victorious determinism.

It is you who are free and can make a choice or remain on the shore and die.

Or the determined course of movement and the eternity of the peopl: flow.

And you see—according Imam Sadiq (ε)—it is neither coercion nor free will but something between these two.

What is the choice of determinism?

Bestowing, bestowing! Obedience and submission (*islam*)!

This great stream of the *ummah*, this eternal flow of people passes the frontier of Mina, it achieves victory in the front against Iblis and the assembled army which begins from Mina's frontier. The sun of the 10th of Dhi-hajjah raises the flag of victory over the tower of dawn and with the first smile, issues both the permission to pass and start on the way—both the command for assault and the start of the battle. Both announces victory and the celebration of the end of duties.

This is the determinism of history, finally, decreed by the multitude.

But in the choice of the human being, finally bestowing of an individual, you.

The if of the ifs is victorious. If you be continuously joined to the flow of the multitude—with the people who resolve upon God—to the *ummah*, this flowing congregation, with the people of this boiling stream, with the Will of fate, the determinism of history. Crush all stones and obstacles before it and—spill it into the sea.

Yea. If to pass through Mash'ar and arrive in Mina, you do not stop upon the way. Do not lose the way. Do not go on your own will. Separate from the congregation. You will arrive in Mina and stone Iblis, sacrifice Ishmael and arrive at the highest peak of your faith and ideal. If you take steps along the path of the people and flow from the same place that the people are flowing; if you mingle your agitation and uproar in order to join the sea with the agitation and uproar of the people in Mash'ar—who spend the night searching for arms and the whispering of love for the next day's *jihad*, for it is a command, an explicit command of God addressed to those who have resolved upon the hajj. *"Then press on from where the people press on."* (2:199)

The army of monotheism, armed and determined, descend into the valley of Mina. The valley of Mina. The place of battle.

STONING THE IDOLS

Three bases, one after another, every base a few hundred meters from the other on a straight line, a route and today—the King's Way—each one a souvenir pillar—a statue, a symbolic form, an idol!

Every year their surfaces are painted white.

Allah akbar! How meaningful.

The invading army arrives at the valley, stones in hand and prepared.

You reach the first idol (*jamarah ula*).

Do not stone it. Pass it by.

You reach the second idol (*jamarah wusta*).

Do not stone it. Pass it by.

You come to the third idol (*jamarah uqba*).

Aim at it; do not pass it by.

Why?

Do not intelligent, logical, experienced advisors, teachers who guide people say: slowly, silently, gradually, sequentially, orderly.

But here Abraham gives the command.

In the first attack, aim at the last one first.

Did you hit it?

Yea!

How many shots?

Seven shots.

Did they definitely hit?

Definitely.

Did you hit its feet and abdomen?

No.

Exactly at its head? Its face? Standing before it?

Yea.

It is finished!

The battle is over. When the last one falls, the first and second cannot remain standing. It is the last which supports the first and second.

The battle is over.

You return from the last front. Other than the sacrifice, you have nothing to do. Announce victory!

The last base falls. Victory.

Celebrate. Come out of the *ihram*. Put on your clothes of life. Use perfume. Adorn yourself. Embrace your marital partner. You are free. A human being. You are victorious over Mina. A conqueror of Iblis.

What am I saying?

You are Abraham.

You have now reached the place where you can sacrifice your Ishmael.

THE SACRIFICE (*qurbani*)

After stoning the last idol, without hesitation, give sacrifice because these three idols are statues in trinity; manifestations of three satanic phases. Do not forget that this is resolving. Be continuously in resolution, conscious of self.

You must know what you are doing and why. Do not become lost in the external form of these rituals. Do not neglect meanings. These are all allusions. Do not remove your eyes—even for a moment—from where you are directed. Do not let formalism bewilder you in the labyrinth of complicated techniques.

Make a hajj of concepts, not just the hajj of rituals.

Here everything relates to intention.

The hajj is totally resolve.

Without an intention, other deeds are perhaps of and by themselves something.

If you do not make your intention known in the ritual fast, you still, at any rate, see an effect from it.

If you do not make your intention known in the *jihad*, you are still a soldier.

But if you do not resolve in the hajj, it is nothing, nothing. It is a series of deeds without benefit for these rituals are all allusions, signs, secrets. "One who knows not the meaning of prostration, only dusts the forehead." "One who realizes not what one is doing in these rituals only brings back gifts from Makkah." Suitcase full, but self, empty:

You act out monotheism in circumambulation in hajj. You express the migration and the efforts of Hagar with the search. From Arafah to Mina, you experience history and the philosophy of the creation of humanity. It is to experience the ascent of the mind from knowledge to love and the ascent of the spirit from earth to heaven until God. And in Mina, the last phase of perfection and idealism, you find absolute freedom, absolute servitude.

Abraham.

Now you are in Mina. You are Abraham. You have brought your Ishmael to the place of sacrifice.

Who is your Ishmael?

What is it?

Your rank? Your reputation? Your position? Your profession? Your wealth? Your home? Your garden? Your automobile? Your beloved? Your family? Your knowledge? Your title? Your art? Your spirituality? Your dress? Your fame? Your sign? Your soul? Your youth? Your beauty...?

How do I know? You know this yourself. You should bring all of it, whatever it is, whoever it is to Mina and chose it for your sacrifice.

I can only give its signs to you: Whatever weakens you upon the way of faith; whatever calls you to stop in your movement; whatever brings doubt to your responsibility; whatever is attached to you and holds you back; whatever you have set your heart upon which does not allow you to hear the message in order to admit the Truth; whatever causes you to flee; whatever leads you towards justification, compromise-seeking hermeneutics and love which makes you blind and deaf.

You are Abraham and the weakness of your Ishmael makes you a plaything of Iblis. You are standing on the highest peak of honor, prevailing with dignity and virtue. There is only one thing in your existence and in order to attain it, you descend from heights. In order not to lose it, you release all of your Abraham-like achievements.

It is your Ishmael. Your Ishmael might be a person or thing, or a state, condition or even a weak point.

But Abraham's Ishmael was his son.

He was an old man in the last days of life. After a century of struggle and mobility , a lifetime filled with migrations, battles, *jihads*, resistances, and entanglements with ignorant tribes; after a lifetime of the oppression of Nimrod, the prejudices of idolatrous custodians, the superstitions of star worshippers and the torture of life, he who had been a liberated, enlightened youth, an upriser in his prejudiced and idol-worshipping and perhaps even idol-making father's house, has now, in his own house, a barren, prejudiced, aristocratic wife: Sarah.

He has now aged. He is alone, bearing the heavy burden of monotheism's mission during a reign of the oppression and ignorance of multitheism, forbearing the torture of a century of "his responsibility to enlighten and liberate," in "an age of darkness with a tribe accustomed to oppression," he has remained a human being at the highest peak of prophethood and a servant of God at the termination of his great Divine mission: He desires to have a son.

But he has a barren wife and he himself is old beyond a hundred years. A person with desires who no longer has hope. Regret and despair fill his soul. God showers Mercy upon His aged, hopeless, lonely, anguished, trustworthy Messenger—His faithful servant who had spent all of his life executing God's Command. God grants Abraham's child, and a son, at that, Ishmael, to the female slave of Sarah, a black woman, who, being of such a lowly class, agitates not the envy of a rival wife.

Ishmael was not only a son for his father Abraham. He was the end of a life of anticipation. He was the reward of a century of suffering, the fruit of an adventurous life, the only young boy of an old father and a glad tiding of hope after bitter despair.

For Abraham, it was Ishmael but your Ishmael might be your 'self'. Perhaps it is your family or position, your wealth, your prestige...how do I know? For Abraham, it was his son and such a son for such a father.

Now, under the rain of caresses and the sun of the love of a father whose life depends upon him, he grows before the eyes of his father—eyes which shine with joy under whitened eyebrows; a father who, like a gardener, only sees the fresh, young sapling in his vast desert and scorched life. It is as if he sees his growing, senses his caresses of love and the warmth of hope in the depths of his soul.

Through the long life of Abraham which had all passed in hardship and danger, these days, the last days of his life, which, according to Gide, "one should drink every moment of with pleasure," are spent with the pleasure of having Ishmael.

The son for whom the father had waited in expectation for one hundred years, who then came at a time when the father was not expecting him, Ishmael had now grown into a strong sapling, a youth, the life of Abraham's soul, the only fruit of Abraham's life and the totality of love, hope and pleasure of Abraham's union.

"Abraham! With your two hands, Place your knife on Ishmael's throat and slaughter him!"

Is it possible to verbally express the horror of the father shocked by this message?

Even if we had been there and had seen, we would not be able to feel it for the magnitude of the pain does not allow the imagination to encompass it.

Abraham, the humble servant of God, the rebellious human of the history of humanity, trembles in fright for the first time in his long life. This steel-like hero of the prophetic mission, melts. This great, idol-destroyer of history is smashed. He is frightened by the horror of the message but the command is the Command of God.

War! The greater war. The war with 'self'. *Jihad akbar* (the greater *jihad*)!

The victor of the greatest war of history is now defeated, weak, frightened, distressed and wretched.

War? The war between God and Ishmael inside Abraham.

The difficulty of choice!

"Who do you choose, Abraham? God or your 'self'? Attachment or values? Union or release? Policy or right? Remaining or advancing? Prosperity or perfection? Pleasure or responsibility? Life for living or life for a goal? Affection and tranquility or ideology and *jihad*? Instinct or consciousness? Emotion or faith? Fatherhood or prophethood? Relationship or Message? And finally, your Ishmael or your God? Choose, Abraham!"

At the end of a century of the Divine Mission among the masses, an entire lifetime under the burden of the prophethood of monotheism and the leadership of the people, the *jihad* against multitheism, the founding of monotheism, the destroying of idols, the eradicating of ignorance, the smashing of pride, the death of tyranny, victorious on all fronts, succeeding in all responsibilities, not hesitating anywhere for self and not being diverted by taking steps for the self, becoming more

Divine-like than any other human being, laying the foundation of monotheism for the *ummah*, pushing forward the leadership of human beings and always, everywhere doing well on all tests...

Do not become proud. Do not rest. Do not think you are a hero, invincible, without weaknesses. Do not be deceived by your one hundred years of *jihad* victories. Do not judge yourself innocent. Do not think yourself immune from the danger of a fall. Do not think yourself above satanic temptations. Do not sense yourself to be invulnerable to the invisible hands that continuously aim at humanness.

The sockets of your eyes are vulnerable to poisoned arrows. Do not assume that you have aged Rostam and confined him. The legendary Simurgh knows you better than you know yourself. It knows you are still vulnerable and penetrable. Covering yourself from head to toe in chain mail, you think that you are invulnerable? You do not know but it knows that there is still an opening to penetrate through, to shoot you with an arrow, to wound and poison you. It will blind you where your eyes are fixed in this world. O invulnerable one! It will darken the world in your eyes by shooting at the very place that you are attached to in this world, from the same rope which attaches you to this world and from the same opening through which you look at the world.

O you hero! You who are standing and boasting! It will destroy you. It will cause your death, for Simurgh is the legendary Rostam's accomplice. It is the collaborator in your fall.

O Abraham! The victorious hero of history's most glorious battle! O invulnerable one! O steel spirit! O you great Messenger of God! Do not think that now that you have come to an end of a century of your Divine Mission, you have traversed the distance between God and man. *"God is closer to you than your jugular vein."* (50:16) The path from mankind to God is the path which lies between primordiality and infinity. What have you been thinking?

You achieved the highest peak of perfection in your mission but you are still imperfect in servanthood. O friend of God! O founder of monotheism upon the earth! O initiator of the way of Moses, Christ and Muhammad (ع)! O symbol of dignity, glory and perfection of human beings! You have become Abraham but it is much more difficult to become a servant of God. You must become absolutely free and absolutely liberated. Do not boast, for one at one's peak is always in danger of falling.

And the fall of one who has reached the highest ascent is the most dangerous and disastrous.

Kill your Ishmael.

Kill him with your own hands.

Take your beloved son, the fruit of your heart, the particle of your soul, the light of your eyes, the fruit of your life, all of your attachment, pleasure, the reason for your existence, everything that has attached you to this life and has held you to it, the meaning of your being, living and staying, your son, no, your Ishmael. Grab him as if he were a sheep to be sacrificed. Lay it on the ground. Hold down its legs to stop its struggling. Grip its fleece. Hold its head firm. Press it to the ground. Twist it back so its jugular vein appears and plays not with the sharp edge of the blade. Amass not the skin of its neck. Bring not pain to the victim. Cut its jugular vein. Keep it under your feet until you feel it no longer moves. Get up from the cold body of your sacrifice and stand by it.

O you who have submitted to the Truth! O servant of God!

This is what the Truth wants from you. This is the invitation of faith and the message of the mission.

This is your responsibility, O responsible human being!

O father of Ishmael.

Now it is Abraham who stands at a crossroad at the end of a long Mission.

His entire soul cries—Ishmael!

And truth pounds at his head—"Slaughter!"

He must choose.

Truth versus interest fight within him: the interest which is attached to his very soul and the Truth which is attached to his faith.

If Truth had asked for his own death, it would have been easy. Abraham has devoted his life to the way of the Truth. This has assured him of being a liberated devotee of Truthand this, for Abraham is a point of weakness.

Whatever is good and beautiful for beautiful spirits and good human beings, for Abraham—the Divine Spirit and exalted human being—is ugly and to be shunned.

Look at the relativity of the 'how' of morality in the school of Abraham and to 'where' it extends.

O one who is beyond self, sacrifice Ishmael!

Doubt!

How painful. How dangerous.

And therefore, procrastination, justification.

At a time when the faith of a human being calls out but the heart is reluctant!

Responsibility calls for a tearing away of the heart from that which the heart cannot easily be torn. He seeks for a means of escape:

And worse than erroneous justifications are correct ones for it means relying on a truth in order to disregard another truth.

And what a tragedy if falsity should take the intellect as a sword in one hand and the Divine Law as a shield in the other!

It is here that the Holy Quran becomes the banner of multitheism and even Ali is disarmed before it and the destiny of Husayn's *ummah* in that of Yazid.

Legitimation!

The worst kind? Rational legitimation.

And the most tragic? Religious legitimation.

Escape from responsibility.

Sacrifice your Ishmael?

Procrastinations, legitimations and justifications: (He wonders): Perhaps this phrase means exactly what it seems to mean. Perhaps the meaning of the word *dhibh'* (slaughter) may be its literal sense. Perhaps it has not been used metaphorically. When it is said, "Kill your ego," it means "abstain from and struggle against the temptations of the ego." Be not a servant to it. Or in the words of a pure Imam, "Die before you die." The word death in the second is perhaps in the literal sense but in the first, the metaphorical. It is a willed death. That is, "Kill your ego."

It is clear that what is meant is: "Remove egotism

from your self." It can, therefore, be concluded that in this phrase, the word *'mut'* does not mean death.

Perhaps the word 'your' in reference to 'your Ishmael' returns particularly to me and in this address, I am the person spoken to. Perhaps here this address is an address to all in general, but it is announced in a particular sense. This can be seen in rhetoric. Examples can be found in the verses, narratives and works of poets.

Perhaps the intent of Ishmael is this very Ishmael, my son. Yet, it might have another metaphorical meaning, another attestation. The word Ishmael might be a general noun or adjective or a word derived from another. It is not improbable that it not have a literal meaning and, in this phrase, not have a specific significance.

Perhaps the phrase "slaughter your Ishmael" is in the objective case; the word Ishmael may be a noun governing the genitive in which the noun has been omitted. This is common in the Arabic language. It can also be seen in the Divine Words. For example, *'sa'l ahl al-ghariyah'* (ask the city) (12:82) means *'sa'l ahl al-ghariyah'* (ask the people of the city) and here the intention behind slaughter Ishmael might be "slaughter your affection for Ishmael."

But suppose we reject these numerous possibilities, that is, suppose we assume that all of these probable meanings are impossible. Suppose we consider the meaning of the words of God to carry the exact sense as the words externally appear to have when they first strike the mind of the listener and that no probable meanings exist. Perhaps the time for the performance of the command and the Will of God Almighty is not right now.

The time for execution has not been set or stipulated in the text of this command. It is evident that this rational principal rules: whatever the Divine Law has not specified and whatever has not appeared in revelation should be entrusted to the intellect. A duty-bound person is obligated to adapt it to the circumstances, interests, conditions of time and place, possibilities and available means and tools.

The command to *jihad* is revealed in the Book but people determine the form of *jihad* according to circumstances and exigencies of the intellect or, in a Tradition, the command has been issued to search for knowledge and it is a religious duty for any religious person. Everyone is appointed to it, but nobody is bound to seek knowledge the moment the duty is given and made obligatory. If at the last moments of life, when one is dying, one takes action to perform this obligation, that person has obeyed the command.

It is similar to the command to hajj that binds the pilgrims-to-be during their lifetime. They leave its performance to a time when they have freely lived and there is no problem in this, either, according to the Divine Law, as this is a duty which should be performed and whenever it is done, it is done because believers conceive of the hajj as something they will each be responsible for on the Day of Resurrection, not in this world. The precepts of the Divine Law are to receive spiritual rewards after death and not to acquire perfection, training, nurturing of the mind and emotions in life before death.

Perhaps this imperative verb, 'slaughter' is an im-

perative command according to the science of principles. A strong possibility is that most certainly it is a
guiding command. It is not like the Quranic phrase, *auto
al-zakat'* which means that people are immediately duty
bound to do so because it is a command of the Master
for in a command of the Master to his servant, the
command of which—that is, performing it —is obligatory upon His servant, it must be immediately obeyed.

Rather, it is like the verse of the Quran, *"And do not
swallow up your property among yourselves by wrongful
means,"* (2:188) whereby God Almighty wished to guide
us by telling us that rulers who wrongfully consume the
property of an orphan commit an ugly act. Therefore the
command in this verse is a guiding one and a guiding
command is a command that even if not mentioned by
the Law-giver, the intellect would deem it to be necessary. In other words, a guiding command is a command
by means of which the Lawgiver makes human beings
aware of the command of the intellect.

Thus, if all other possibilities are negated, commen-
taries and hermeneutics, so much is certain that what
God Almighty wishes by the phrase,*"And know that your
possessions and your children are a test,"* (8:28) is that
"affection for one's children is a test" and the meaning
of what was understood is a universal truth. One should
be in perfect submission before God and leave aside
everything. Even the dearest concerns in life should not
create obstacles in one's uniting with God and/or
become tools to occupy one in order to distance one
from God. And as Ishmael attracted much of the affection of Abraham, this affection was forbidden through
the revealed words with the word 'slaughter' because a

strong affection for children preoccupies the servant of God and prevents the remembrance of God.

The purpose of forbidding this act, which is a guiding forbiddance, is to make Abraham aware of the fact that his affection towards Ishmael prevented his spirit and heart from submitting completely to the Truth and allowed him to love something other than He. The fact has been proven elsewhere that the intention behind "slaughter Ishmael" is "slaughter the affection for Ishmael." And the verse, "*And know that your possessions and your children are a test,*" (8:28) is in this sense.

And the final procrastination and justification, all of these intellectual and *shari'ah* categories, documented by the holy verses, narratives, reasonings of theology, principles, citations to the intellect and documentary evidence of the past, negate this command for it is contrary to the Divine Law. It is impossible to attest a command to a sin and a forbidden act to God.

Yea. Justification. Legitimation. Rationalization. Looking for a means of escape when responsibility become heavy and incompatible with what a person wants. When a 'truth' enhances one's material life, many people become seekers of 'truth'. The 'truth' can be satisfied by performing acts of charity, hand in hand with business, work, transactions in the bazaar and a nice, sweet, undisturbed, comfortable life.

When a truth is placed in the midst of the flow and course of one's life, it itself becomes a stock-in-hand and capital for business. It brings bread and water and consequently: a profession, an official, legalized profession which offers bread and water, fame and title. Then every person becomes both a longer for truth and a fanatic believer as well as having the hope of being a source of service and a possessor of influence upon this way.

But when a truth confronts life and the seeking of truth develops inconveniences, difficulties, loss and danger... when the road is an up-hill one, full of stones and sharp cliffs and there are many places to be ambushed by plunderers, when the weather is stormy and the night is dark and frightening, when companions are few in number and with every step, they decrease and finally alone!

When tearing away your heart from all attachments that call you to stay at the bottom of the valley , when harmonizing yourself with nations and tribes accustomed to darkness in the valley who have all come to terms with each other, when the message of truth tells you to tear your heart away from the Ishmael of your fame, grade, soul and love and to go ahead but the temptation of the heart tells you to stay, to halt, to get along with each other, here the final deceit of the human being, who is both conscious and responsible, is justification—searching for a solution both to halt and to remain but to somehow or another narcotize the conscience; to choke the voice of reproach in the 'self'; to so alter and distort religion that it becomes harmonious with the world; to preserve one's Ishmael but not in such a way as others do who are condemned for denying rights and rebelling against God, who commit treason against the people, who drink wine with the intention of drinking sweetened water or with the intention of taking medicine.

Justification means to give a rightful visage to something which is not rightful. You can name this justification what you like—jurisprudential, religious, commonsensical, commonly practiced, ethical, practical, psychological, sociological, dialectical, intellectual...

But, on the hajj, God has termed it satanic justification and in the fate of the great Abraham, at that, the old man Abraham, victorious in all his tests: in his sincerity, piety, knowledge, action, anguish, *jihad* and absolute longing for the Truth.

One of these obvious 'perhaps' is to seize the powerful intellect and firm and pure sincerity of Abraham: "I heard this message while asleep. Perhaps..."

Iblis kindles affection for the child in Abraham's heart; blows a 'logical reason' into his intellect.

The first time

Stoning the first idol

He refrains from carrying out the command and keeps his Ishmael.

*****

"O Abraham, slaughter your Ishmael."

This time, the command, more direct, more decisive. The war rages within Abraham. The great hero of history is helpless and subject to distress, doubt, fear and weakness.

The standard bearer of the great mission of monotheism has become a plaything of Iblis? He is crushed in the struggle between God and Iblis. Pain has set fire to his bones.

Human existence: oppositions in the depth of one's existence intellect and love, consciousness and conscience, life and faith, self and God!

Humanity. This intermediate link between animal and angelic being, nature and God, instinct and consciousness of self, earth and heaven, world and future life, love of self and love of God, reality and truth, pleasure and virtue, remaining and advancing, presence and absence, to be and to become, captivity and salvation, deliverance and responsibility, tendency towards self and tendency towards God, multitheism and monotheism.

'For me' and 'for us'... And finally, that which exists and that which must be.

*****

It is the second day. The weight of responsibility and the rapture of desire exceeds the day before. Ishmael has fallen into danger and Abraham keeping him, more difficult. Iblis must employ greater vigilance, logic and skill to deceive Abraham, deceit from the same forbidden fruit which it made Adam eat of.

Abraham: a human being, this gathering of contradictions, the front of light and darkness, good and evil, the combination of putrid clay and Spirit, bad smelling swamp and Divine Spirit, this soul, *"That which inspired it to lewdness and piety!"* (91:8) Abraham now: a doubt, a vacillation, a choice, that is all! Kinship or the Message?

O Messenger of God! O responsible! O Messenger to the people, do you wish to remain the father of your Ishmael?

But...slaughter my Ishmael? With my own hands?
Yea!
Yea! You must overlook your Ishmael for God. The responsibility to ideology is superior to the responsibil-

ity to emotion.

The invitation of the message or the pleasure of being a father?

Iblis kindles love for the child in his heart and blows a 'logical reason' into his intellect.

"But ...I heard the message in my sleep. Perhaps..."

The second time.

Stone the middle idol.

He refrains from carrying out the command to slaughter Ishmael and keeps him, instead.

"O Abraham! Slaughter your Ishmael."

More direct and more decisive.

The work of justification becomes more difficult as the illumination of truth and the pressure of responsibility are more direct and heavier than to be able to escape.

Abraham is so situated in such narrow circumstances that he senses a doubt in the message which is no longer justification. It is treason. The limits of growth and depravity have appeared so decisively and explicitly before his eyes that even the power and genius of Iblis are no longer effective in making sophistic statements.

Abraham senses that in denying this message, he has confessed to Iblis.

At the edge of a fall over a sharp cliff.

The fall of Abraham, the idol-destroyer Abraham, the great Messenger of God, the founder of Islam and the leader of the people.

From the highest peak of monotheism (*tawhid*) to the most inferior swam of multitheism (*shirk*).

And what am I saying?

Multitheism (*shirk*). No. Multitheism means multiple gods, the worshipping of others with God.

And now, in the language of the Quran when it refers to worship, monotheism and multitheism, Abraham stands at the edge of worshipping Iblis instead of God! Because now quite clearly Iblis, in the front of Mina, stands face to face with Allah.

There is no way to come to terms with both. There is no way to pull back from both. No co-existence, no neutrality. O how difficult and frightening is this tale.

And the human being, this Divine-like figure of the world, who can bring the universe under his command, how impotent!

He has the Spirit of God within him and yet *"is created weak."* (4:28) He is not immune from fall in any position.

In life, as a child who is just beginning to walk, he must watch out for himself at the edge of a cliff. Even the Seal of Prophets of monotheism—Muhammad, peace and the mercy of God be upon him and his household—who is the greatest infallible person—if he had not watched himself, he would have stumbled and given whatever he had accomplished to the winds. Even he was not safe from multitheism.

Abraham, father of the Prophets, endowed with resolve, killer of multitheism, destroyer of idols in the history of man, in the last phase of his life, and at the highest peak of his human power and Divine glory, only his affection for his son has brought him to the edge of Iblis' cliff.

The most powerful hero of monotheism and father of God's Prophets, after living a century as Abraham, and adorned head to toe with Divine signs, glory and certainty, now, a bewildered plaything of Iblis.

O Abraham! No solution has been left to you. God and satan are on either side of you. Whom do you choose, Abraham?

The final proof has come for Abraham. He has no doubt that his message is the message of what is right. He has no doubt about the certainty in the message, for uncertainty is satanic.

He can still create a logical reason. His logical reason is still valid, but his conscience makes mockery of him. He senses and finds the illumination and warmth of what is right in the depths of his primordial nature, in his emotions, his whole being like an inflamed particle of fire.

That which is right, the Truth, is much stronger, more explicit and closer than to require intellectual reasons. The man of truthfulness feels it as the radiation of the sun. As he finds the existential self. He consciencizes the existence of Truth.

The human being who longs for what is right has a sixth sense about his Lord, a sharp sense which never errs. It is like a honey bee who searches and finds its invisible way to its beehive by a mysterious power of orientation from distances of hundreds of kilometers, over thousands of mountains and valleys, in the midst of obstacles of darkness and storms and through innumerable mountainous routes and minor paths, overland and overseas. The human being who knows the Truth, finds God in this way and recognizes the direction in the midst of nights and storms, conspiracies and thousands of temptations, magicians... and Abraham, commander of the longers for the Truth of history, has spent his long life in longing for the Truth, doing what is right, has grown upon the way of seeking the Truth, gained maturity and been nourished and now, is it possible that he not re-recognize the message of Truth and not understand the temptations of Iblis?

Although a friend has now lit a fire for him which is more frightening and inflammable than the fire that the enemy had lit and although the enemy strives now to have the fire grow cold within him and appear to be a red rose, the criteria of friend and enemy, Truth and falsehood are not considered as to what they do to you. These two relate to other criteria which are beyond profit and loss to you or me.

Abraham is now aware of what to do. With certainty, he has realized the purpose of the message. He understands that all such uncertainties were efforts of satan from the very beginning. The indescribable love of an aged father who, after a long life of anticipation and despair until he fathered a child, drives him unconsciously towards such justifications and uncertainties in order to find a way of escape, a solution to perhaps help him, without confronting God or disobeying His order, to keep Ishmael. But now everything is clear and explicit.

Anguish! Anguish!

Ah, what tragedy. How frightening.

Abraham is responsible. Yea. He now knows it well but his duty is more bitter and more difficult than to be held in the mind of a father and that for such an aged father alone—like Abraham.

And to slaughter one's only son, at that, like Ishmael. If it were only the slaughter of Abraham at the hands of Ishmael, how easy! What a pleasure! But no! The young Ishmael must die and the old, aged Abraham must remain, alone, sad and bereaving...With his aged, bloody hands!

Whenever Abraham thinks about the message, he thinks of nothing except submission and he no longer has any uncertainty. The message is the message of God and Abraham, this great rebel of history yields absolutely before Him!

But when he thinks about performing the command and slaughtering his Ishmael, helplessness and impotency so crush him under the pressure that his exalted stature bends as a lantern folds into itself. Sadness wrinkles this clear face which is a mirror of purity and forbearance like a burned piece of leather and under a mountain of pain, darkness. It seems as if he hears the sounds of the breaking of his bones.

And Iblis who sees the sovereignty of weakness, helplessness and fear all over the soul of Abraham and sees what pain does to him, covets him, for Iblis—the revengeful enemy from the moment since the Fall of Adam upon the earth, lies in ambush for Adam's children—is present wherever he smells human scent. He begins to work wherever he finds traces of fear, weakness, uncertainty, despair, envy, selfishness, foolishness and even great affection towards something. Bad things are good stocks for Iblis so that if something holds your feet from moving, he calls you to it and prevents you from doing your duty. He attempts to darken and weaken the explicit message of God in your heart, of affection for a child. "*And know that your possessions and your children are a test (fitnah).*" (8:28)

What is *fitnah* The test furnace, the obstacle in the course of belief and Ishmael is Abraham's only attachment, his only weak point before Iblis.

Now, Abraham has deserted affection for Ishmael. The message is the Message of Truth. In his heart, the anguish of losing Ishmael has filled the place of the pleasure in keeping him. Sorrow has attached itself to the soul of Abraham like an angry hyena and eats him out from within. The scent of grief intoxicates Iblis and brings him joy. Grief in human beings makes them delicious mouthfuls for the claws and teeth of Iblis.

Iblis again gains hope and covets the sorrowful Abraham. He comes to him in his disguise. He appears in the depths of his unconscious consciousness and repeats again what he had said twice before.

The logic of Iblis is always the same: the repetition of one thing, although in hundreds of colors and with a variety of tricks. "I...this message in my sleep!"

But no. That's enough. That's enough Abraham.

Abraham makes his decision. He makes his choice. It is clear what Abraham's choice is. Which one? The absolute freedom of servitude to God. Sacrificing Ishmael, the last bond that binds him to servitude to himself. He decides to first tell his son his story. He calls his son. His son comes forward. The father looks at the elevated stature of his sacrifice. Ishmael, this great sacrifice.

*****

Now in Mina, in the stony solitude of that corner of the earth, a conversation between a father and a son. A father who has a head of snow white hair and more than a century has passed over his weakened body. And a son, newly blooming and fragile.

The sky of the peninsula...What am I saying? The sky of the world lacks the strength to observe this scene. History is unable to listen. Never before on earth has such a conversation taken place between two people, a father and a son, not even in the imagination. A conversation so intimate and so frightening, it would appear that the father has not the strength to tell the story and express the struggles in his spirit. He is even unable to express in words: "I have been appointed to slaughter you with my own hands." He leaves his heart to God, grits his teeth and says:

"*My son, I see in a dream that I shall sacrifice thee.*" (37:101) These words are hurriedly tossed out of his mouth so that he not hear them, not listen to them and so that they would quickly come to an end. They ended and he remained silent with a frightening visage, a horrified look for he feared looking at Ishmael.

Ishmael, realizing his father's pitiful state, consoles him. "*My father, dost as thou art bidden; thou shalt find me, insha'llah, among the steadfast.*" (37:102)

Abraham has now found a wondrous strength, with a will which no longer seeks to be pulled by anything but a longing for the Truth which is nothing other than absolute freedom. With a decisive determination, he arises to the arising, so nimble that he once and for all makes Iblis despair. Ishmael—the young man of monotheism—who is nothing other than absolute freedom, with a will which no longer seeks to be pulled by any force but the longing for Truth—in surrender to the Truth— has become so softened and tamed that he appears as a calm and patient sacrifice!

The father takes the knife and with an indescribable power, places it upon a stone to sharpen it. Is this how he shows his fatherly affection towards the dearest thing in life? Is this the only affection he can give his son?

First he kills his inner 'self' with the power that loves, the power that gives spirit. He lets loose the jugular vein of his soul, empties himself of self and fills self with love of God.

A living being who breathes only for God!

Then he rises to the power of God and leads his young victim, who is standing calmly and silently, towards the place of sacrifice. He lays him on the ground, keeping him under his nimble hands and feet. He puts his face to the stone. He grips a handful of his hair and pushes it back a bit. His jugular vein jumps out. He yields himself to God and places the knife on the throat of his victim, squeezing the handle with an angry power and in great haste. All efforts of the old man are focused on this point so that all of it will come to an end and he will be freed before he becomes conscious and opens his eyes to see.

But!

Alas! The knife!

This knife does not cut. It brings pain. What an unmerciful torture.

He throws his knife down upon the stone in anger. He roars like a wounded lion in pain. Anger and anguish struggle within him. He becomes frightened. He becomes apprehensive of his fatherhood. He jumps quickly, grabs the knife and again rushes towards his victim who is calm, silent, motionless.

When suddenly...a sheep...and a Message which says, *"Abraham, thou hast confirmed the vision; thus do We reward the good-doers. This is indeed the manifest trial."* (37:105-6) *"Allahu akbar.*

This means that the sacrifice of a human being for God, which was a common religious tradition in the past and a form of ritual, is forbidden. In the nation of Abraham, a sheep is sacrificed for a human being and more meaningful than this, namely that the God of Abraham is not thirsty like gods are thirsty for blood. It is the servants of gods who are hungry, hungry for meat!

And more meaningful than this. From the very beginning, God did not want Ishmael to be slaughtered! He wanted Abraham to be the slaughterer of Ishmael. And so he became—so bravely.

The slaughter of Ishmael is now useless. From the beginning, God wanted Ishmael to be the slaughter of God and it happened. How patiently. Again, the sacrifice of Ishmael is useless.

Here we are not speaking about 'the needs of God'. Words everywhere refer to the 'needs of mankind'. And such is the wisdom of God, the Wise and Kind Who loves human beings...Who raised Abraham to the highest peak of his sacrificing his Ishmael without sacrificing Ishmael...Who promotes Ishmael to the highest position of being the great sacrifice of God, without bringing any harm to him.

The story of this religion is not the story of the torture or torment of human beings and the thirst of gods for blood. The story concerns the perfection of humanity, freedom from the prison of instinct, freedom from the narrow straits of selfishness, the elevation of

the spirit, the ascension of love, the miraculous authority of mankind's will power and salvation from any
prison or relationship that captivates it and weakens its
position in the name of being a responsible human being
before the Truth. And finally, arriving at the highest
station of martyrdom. Ishmael-like.

And greater than martyrdom? That which still has
no definition in the dictionary of humanity—Abraham-
like.

And the end of the story? The sacrifice of a sheep.

And what God seeks for Himself in this greatest
human tragedy? The sacrifice of sheep for a number of
hungry.

And now, you who have arrived in Mina, you must
have Abraham-like brought your sacrifice. You must
have chosen your Ishmael from the beginning for sacrifice.

Who is your Ishmael? What is it? It is not necessary
that anyone else know. Only you must know and God.
Your Ishmael might not be your child or your only son.
It might be your wife, your husband, your occupation,
your fame, your passion, your power, your situation,
your position. I do not know. Anything in your eyes
which holds the place of Ishmael in the eyes of Abraham.

Whatever has become an obstacle to your performing your responsibility for the Truth, has enchained
your freedom, has become an attachment for pleasure
which calls you to remain with your "self", which has,
like a chain of society, tied you firmly to the ground,
does not let you go. The same thing which makes you an
accomplice of Iblis if you keep it. That everything which
deafens your ears before the Message of Truth, which

darkens your understanding, which infects your heart. Whatever justifies rebellion before the command of faith and fleeing from a heavy and difficult responsibility. Whatever and whoever keeps you behind in order for you to maintain it.

These are the signs of Ishmael. Search for them in yourself, in your lifetime; pick them up; slaughter them in Mina now that you have attempted to move towards God.

Do not personally select the sheep from the beginning but let God make the selection and grant it to you in place of the slaughter of your Ishmael. It is this way that He accepts the slaughter of a sheep as a sacrifice from you. The slaughtering of a sheep instead of Ishmael is a sacrifice. The slaughter of a sheep as a sheep is butchery.

THE TRINITY OF IDOLS

Now, have you recognized these three idols in Mina? These three manifestations of Iblis who tempted Abraham? Does the human being not pass through three phases from the time that it uproots the self until it moves on the ascent towards absolute freedom and breaks all enslaving bonds and attachments in becoming a total Divine-like being? Moves through the animal phase of existence for 'self' but with others—respectability. This is sublimated in the phase of Abrahamic existence for God but with self-authenticity.

Are these three idols not the three secret negative phases which in this present, greater hajj are positively symbolized by Arafah (knowledge), Mash'ar (consciousness) and Mina (love)?

Does the first idol not oppose knowledge (Arafah), the middle idol, consciousness (Mash'ar) and the last, love, faith (Mina)?

I have no further powers of thought. My understanding does not extend beyond this. But this question must be answered: exactly what do these three idols do, these three principles and powerful factors of Iblis which prevent 'becoming Abraham-like', waiting in ambush for human beings and not allowing them to perform their Divine Mission?

They negate and metamorphosize the Message of Truth. By relying on the human being's strongest attachments, which are the greatest points of weakness and the stumbling blocs in causing their fall, they paralyze them and prevent them from moving towards perfection and doing what is right.

Another sign which they have which helps us in finding the objective identity alluding to them is that these three idols are three independent idols; each has a name, title and base but all three are accomplices and all three follow the same course; all three stand before the way of a responsible human being and a human being upon the way.

Most important of all, although all three are independent beings, they are manifestations of one existence: Iblis. A single existence, but, at the same time, three. They are three existences and, at the same time, one.

It is amazing that this is the prevalent definition of a trinity: three gods. In the Jewish faith, there are three hypostasis as Philo said. In Christianity: Father, Son and

Holy Ghost. In Greece: three visages in a single head. In India: Vishu—three visages, as well, in a single head. In Hinduism: Meno in three essences: head, hand and chest. In ancient Iran: Ahura Mazda in three fires, Gushtasp, Istakhr and Barzinmehr. And in another place: mediator of God, shadow of God and sign of God.

What is multitheism (*shirk*)? The earthly religion: rightly declared by the scientific philosophy of history as being the offspring of society's foundation, the justifier of the status quo, the supra-structure which compromises with the materialistic foundation of a society and, consequently, the narcotizer of the people's consciousness of self.

This is true and more true than has been understood by those who have expressed it—but in relation to the religion of multitheism. The religion of monotheism opposes multitheism and cannot be born of the same thing or have the same essence or role. The way of history is the war of religion against religion, monotheism versus multitheism. But they have turned the social realization of the religion of monotheism into multitheism—multitheism hidden in the disguise of monotheism which is even more dreadful...and more durable.

The trinity of Christianity has been monotheism. Are not Vishu and Ahura, etc., one god?

I believe all religions were based on monotheism and when, in the course of history, the social system was changed to multitheism, when the original classless societies were changed into ones which class distinctions and multi-groups, monotheism changed into multitheism.

From Adam two sons remained. Two human beings: Cain, the landlord, killed his brother, Abel, the herder. No one has spread the news of Cain's death because Cain has not died as yet. He who became Adam's heir was a usurper, a murderer, who committed fratricide, a worshipper of lust; a landowner in rebellion against God and successor not worthy of Adam. The children of Adam who ruled history are the children of Cain.

Society grew. Institutions and disciplines became complex. Thus, classification, specialization and divisions came into being. Cain, the ruling power, the appointing force, usurper of rights and owner of everything appeared in three visages because in an advanced society, politics, economics and religion were expressed in three dimensions. Cain leaned on all three bases separately. He created the three powers of coercion, wealth and asceticism. And from these three, despotism, exploitation and deception appeared. Monotheism calls the three manifestations of them: Pharaoh, Karun and Balam b. Ba'ur. But multitheism justifies these three gods of the earth in its three dimensional system of ruling through religion and it named them three gods in the heavens.

These three gods call you from servitude to God to servitude to them. O you who put on the dress of Abraham! These lead you to the 'worship of Ishmael' so that they themselves dominate over you. They place your neck in a rope, empty your pockets, paralyze your intellect and lead you into darkness.

Strike! O you who have come to Mina!

O you who have brought Ishmael to the place of sacrifice!

Like Abraham, stone Iblis in each of its three visages.

O follower of that great idol-destroyer and soldier of monotheism, destroy all three idols!

With the rising of the sun of the 10th of Dhihajjah, attack the place of *jamarah* at the moment which time itself has announced, step in step with the *ummah*, with the multitude of wearers of *ihram*, setting out from Mash'ar, pass through the borders of Mina. In the first attack, stone the last one!

Indeed, who is the last that it should be destroyed first? Pharaoh? Karun? Or Balam b. Ba'ur? These three idol-statues of Cain's power and three manifestations of Iblis are multitheism's trinity against monotheism.

Aim at Pharaoh for *"judgement is only God's"* (6:57)

Aim at Karun for wealth belongs to God. (24:33)

Aim at Balam b. Ba'ur for *"religion should only be for God."* (8:39)

The representatives of God in nature are people. The Family of God on the earth are people and the earth is inherited by His virtuous servants.

That is, the sovereignty of God is in the hands of the people. And all capital belongs to the people. And they are totally responsible for God's religion—people!

Among these three, which one is Pharaoh that one worships coercion? Which one is Karun that one worships wealth? Which one is Balam b. Ba'ur that one worships the temple?

Every Abrahamic intellectual who possesses cognitive insight and a method for social struggle sees one of them to be more essential than the others according to the social order for which he is responsible.

A political combatant believes Pharaoh to be the last

idol which is stoned first who prevails in a despotic, military and fascist system. An economic thinker who believes the economic factor to be the determining force knows Karun to be the last. A *mujahid* thinker, an intellectual combatant who sees ignorance, intellectual solidification and factors which cause sleep and which suffocate awareness, consciousness of self and growth to be in the religion of multitheism or metamorphosized monotheism and who believe that as long as minds are not moved, nothing will move, consider the last one to be Balam b. Ba'ur.

Upon the first two or three of my journeys, I considered Balam b. Ba'ur to be the last and stoned aiming at Balam, in particular since I found the Quran in agreement with this choice for it mostly attacks hypocrisy, multitheism, ignorance and it objects to the worship of pseudo-clergymen. *"Take they their divine and monks as lords beside God?"* (9:31) And the sharp, angry tone, in particular to pseudo-religious scholars who *"were placed under the Pentateuch and they followed it not, is as the similitude of a donkey bearing books."* (62:5) *"And their similitude is like the parable of a dog; if you attack him, he lolls out his tongue and if you leave him alone, he lolls out his tongue."* (7:176)

And in the last chapter where the Quran comes to an end, my opinion is wondrously confirmed with a marvelous statement, with the power and beauty of the Divine words. The verse is addressed to the person of the Prophet. Where the Quran ends, it tells this great personality, the master of the greatest Divine Mission and the one responsible for leadership, consciousness and the salvation of mankind, "You are not secure from an evil. Take refuge in God."

Where it speaks about God, it introduces Him with three characteristics. *"Say, 'I take refuge with the Lord of the people, the King of the people, the Deity of the people."* (114:1-3)—the negation of these three powers, which were exclusively God's alone, and which the three idols took unto themselves alone.

We see that here, pseudo divine and spiritual powers have come at the end (of the Quran). Even a person such as the Prophet must take refuge in the Lord of the people, the King of the people and the Deity of the people and from whom? From the evil of whom? The evil of *khanas*. Who is *khanas*? The Holy Quran clearly specifies, *"From the evil of the temptations of satan (khanas) who whispers in the breasts of the people."* (114:4-5)

We see the words are referring to a power which brings temptation into the hearts, thoughts, sensations and beliefs of the people. And in Mina, it is Iblis who is relevant, who projected temptation into the heart of Abraham.

Therefore, the last one is this very satanic *khanas*... the pseudo-spiritual man who sells his religion, the pseudo-scholar who sells his knowledge, the intellectual who commits treason. According to the Quran, the first factor causing segregation, perversion and oppression in the history of humanity that leads the uncontradicted and classless society for the first time into discrepancy and discrimination because *"people are but one ummah,"* (2:213) are those who consider themselves responsible for religion, religious sciences and are the executors of religious and Divine Laws who had come to eliminate discrepancies, dispersions and contradictions and all of this, not because of religious prejudices and intellectual differences and not unconsciously, either! But consciously and because of aggression, oppression and envy.

People all formed a single group, equal and classless society, without contradiction and discrepancy. *"And God sent Prophets as bearers of good tidings and warners and sent down with them the Book with the Truth that it might judge between men in that which they differed and none differed therein but those very (people) whom it was given unto after clear signs had come onto them through revolt among themselves."* (2:213)

But this hajj is more profound and richer than my understanding can comprehend. Every time I went, I thought I understood all of it and the next journey would only be repetitious. But on the next journey, I was surprised how little I understood about the hajj on my previous journey.

And you, my reader, do not think that what I have said of the hajj covers all meanings of the hajj, senses the richness of the hajj. No. What I really claim is that this is my understanding of the hajj. You must strive yourself to understand it in another way. This is not a practical treatise about the rituals but a reflective one. This reflects the strength of a normal mind which has attempted to analyze this miraculous secret drama where the stage manager is He Who Manages the universe. It may seem that I have attempted to pour the ocean into a cup!

It is because of this that on every journey I corrected my previous understanding and completed previous comments and I found new secrets and added new points. Thus my explorations and witnessing in relation to the previous journey were everything and in relation to the next, nothing.

On my last journey I thought to myself: Why should I specify that which the Stage Manager has not specified? If they should have been specified, He would have done so. As He has not specified these three, this is itself a specification—are all three not one and one in three?

Thus specification of these three idols causes the mind to separate those three dimensions which are inseparable. Because of this, He has not specified them so that it can be said that in each idol, the others are hidden and with every stoning, resolve to stone the other two as well!

Moreover, it is the moulded minds of people, the minds of philosophers and scholars who carve fixed frameworks and monotonous standards which they call sociology, the philosophy of history and psychology— the Creator of the hajj knows that in every cultural and civilized period, in every historical phase, in every social order, in every productive infrastructure, class fabric, intellectual superstructure and mass communications, one of these three powers is the ruling power and preserves the other two. Consequently, the negating of it becomes the factor for salvation, the essence of victory and the *eid* of Sacrifice. One must, therefore, consider it to be the last idol in Mina and in the first attack, it should be put under a rain of stones.

It is because of this that the intention of the stone thrower who comes from a developed, capitalistic country differs from that of one who comes from a declining, religious Middle Ages society or a person who comes from a fascist or individual dictatorial system although all three are the same and the last one holds the other two within because Pharaoh makes plundering legal for Karun and Balam makes it into canonical law. Karun keeps the system of Balam going by the power of wealth and Pharaoh supports it with coercion. Balam keeps the pillars of power of Pharaoh upon the shoulders of gods in heaven and Karun keeps them under the feet of gods of the earth. We see that each of them firmly holds their twin at their side with their two arms while holding itself up, helps the other two to stand. You who come from all parts of the world, during whatever era of time, hit the last one with the intention of all three, with the intention your Abraham had, responsibility which is expedient among your nation because as you reject Iblis, in his last deception, you automatically negate all his previous deceptions.

For humanity is always the victim of the last deceit.

Did you hit the last one? Face to face? On the head? Did you hit it? Seven shots?

The number of the days when the creation of the world came to an end. The number of planets. The seven heavens. Seven days of the week. That is, a *jihad* in harmony with time as the universe itself. Does it refer to a battle begun at the beginning of creation? Is it in harmony with nature?

What am I saying? That is, innumerable. That is, always, without end, without concession, peace or compromise. Without a cease-fire. There can be no peaceful co-existence with idols. That is why your lifetime should continuously be spend in Mina (love, faith), throwing stones. Because seven is a number of multiplicity.

The last one falls. O Abraham! Iblis has fallen to its knees, paralyzed under your determined and continuous stoning. And you, O human being! O vice-gerent of God on earth! You, also expelled Iblis as the Divinity had done.

You threw before your feet the only angel who rebelled against prostrating before you, with your Abraham-like power, became free, became Abraham! You who were a plaything of Iblis, worshipper of an idol, now, all angels prostrate before you.

You have now achieved the Station of Abraham. You hear the message and recognize the command. You return victorious from the last field of Battle. When you destroyed the last idol, you achieved the position of having slaughtered your 'Ishmael' upon the way of love. Now you can intend to slaughter your 'Ishmael' upon the way of longing for the Truth.

You return from stoning the last idol, victorious, love in your heart, a freed servant of Truth, you resolve to slaughter with determined feet.

And you step in the footsteps of Abraham, the Ishmael of your life in one hand and the knife of your faith in the other until you reach the place of sacrifice and throw down your Ishmael upon the earth. Before the feet of your decision. Before your truth-seeking eyes.

You grit your teeth and tie your heart to God.

O you who have all become Truth! O you who have come to Mina! Place your knife upon the throat of your Ishmael.

And..

Cut the head of a sheep for the God of Abraham is not thirsty for blood and does not need your Ishmael. All these were to bring you here. To bring you out of your dark home. O victim of the three shadows of Iblis! To the place of sacrifice of Mina, O monotheist idol-destroyer!

And now, O you who have placed the knife on the throat of Ishmael upon the way of God! And have come to Mina to kill your Ishmael but now your hands are soaked with Iblis' blood and your Ishmael, full of glory, is by your side.

In slaughtering Ishmael you are now able to stone Iblis.

Whoever is able to bring Iblis to its knees must first free the self from the ties of the Ishmael of self. Thus the situation is reversed. As long as the anxiety of Ishmael exists within you, Iblis stands erect in Aqabah.

How amazing! What lessons are taught to a person in this mountainous environment.

Now you become Abraham. You have thrown Iblis to the ground. Bring back your Ishmael from the place of sacrifice. What you should have slaughtered was not Ishmael. It was your attachment to Ishmael. Iblis' pretext, Ishmael is himself the beloved of God and the gift of God, the gift God bestowed upon you and now it is God who pays personally for its ransom.

Bring back your Ishmael from the place of sacrifice. Return together from the front of Mina, from the place of God's covenant. Carry forward Abraham's monotheistic mission upon your shoulders. Go towards the people to establish the sacred land, the sacred time, the sacred society, the clear and secure sanctuary of God, building the house of liberty for the people: the secure, liberated shelter of equality and love!

THE FESTIVAL OF SACRIFICE (*eid*)

Now everything is coming to an end. The hajj has come to its end. Where? In Mina. O wonder! Behind the wall of Makkah. Mina is wall to wall with Makkah. It is in a suburb of Makkah, a few steps from the Ka'bah.

Why did the hajj end before reaching the Ka'bah? Why not in Makkah, in the Masjid al-Haram or the Ka'bah? And why in Mina?

You must understand this secret. You must understand all of the secrets of the hajj. You must meditate on what you have done. Not deliberations in the solitude of self but in a congregation within a congregation.

Moreover, the hajj relies upon a congregation. Here is the place of the covenant of God with Abraham, Muhammad, peace be upon him, and the people.

People who have come from all parts of the world, people of different colors, different nationalities, different languages, different countries and different rules. But all enjoy one culture, one faith, one history, one ideal and love.

Every group is a natural and free representative of a nation and not officially selected, carrying a written command. Each person has come from the intimate fabric of the people, common people of the bazaar, farms and centers of education.

There is no stipulation as to class, occupation, personality, knowledge and wealth. Being able means having the power to perform the hajj and not necessarily to be wealthy. The hajj is not a tax on wealth. It is a duty, a duty like the ritual prayer for it requires having the ability which is a logical requirement just as the power to perform any other duty is required.

Here all true representatives of nations are assembled with their own particular sorrows and sorrows common to all.

THE PAUSE AFTER THE FESTIVAL

A time for ideology and a time for action. Today, the 10th of Dhihajjah, the *eid* of Sacrifice, the hajj has come to an end, but you must stay in Mina for the 11th and 12th. You may not leave Mina. The 13th you are free to stay in Mina if you want.

On these three days, it is forbidden to leave Mina. You are not even permitted to leave at night to circumambulate the Ka'bah. Why? Because the stoning has ended. The sacrifice is over. We have changed out of our *ihram*. We have celebrated. All the restrictions of being in the *ihram* have ended.

Then why should a million human beings stay behind the gate of this town and in this dry valley for three days? To sit and meditate on the hajj. We must expound all we have done and understand it.

We should sit and discuss our pains, needs, difficulties and ideals with our fellow-sympathizers, fellow-sufferers, fellow-companions who have gathered here from all parts of the world with the warmth from the same love, having been illuminated with the same faith. Scholars from Muslim countries, responsible intellectuals from all continents of the world, Muslim *mujahid*s entangled in their countries with colonialism, exploitation, cruelty, poverty, ignorance, superstition, hypocrisy and corruption should come to know each other, discuss problems and seek each other's assistance.

Muslims of the world should study the world of Islam and Islam, in this, their contemporary age. Plan and discuss the common dangers, conspiracies against them and the enmity of the great powers of the world and their internal agents. Find solutions. They should prepare a plan for a world-wide campaign against efforts of dispersion, blind prejudice, black waves of propagation, dispersion of superstitions which nourish ignorance, poisonous sprays of the feelings of revenge, the spirit of secularism, innovation, deviated tendencies, religious invention, cultural destruction and hundreds of other colorful diseases that threaten the *ummah*. They should aim at achieving Islamic goals, human ideals, the liberty of enslaved nations, captive and oppressed Muslim minorities in fascistic, prejudiced political and religious regimes, the creation of the spirit of harmony, understanding, correlation of ideas and emotions, the strengthening of unity against common enemies as well as plans to eliminate scientific, intellectual and jurisprudential discrepancies between Islamic sects, reducing the distance, the differences, rightly coming to recognize and understand each other through discussions and disputes, true free discussions and a study of different views, and, in the light of the encounter of ideas and opinions, in searching for the Truth, find a way to the original source of Islam.

A three day forced pause of a million representatives of Muslims of the world behind the wall of Makkah in Mina. In this mountainous valley where there is nothing special to see and nothing to do, no bazaar to do business, no park for recreation and not even a habitable place to live in. Nothing. Even the construction of a building in Mina is prohibited by the command of the Prophet.

In these moments when the hajj frees everyone from ties and attachments to individual life, when the penetration of the powerful spirit of Abraham, in the personality of those who have assumed his role, have washed away fears, passions and weaknesses from the spirits, have agitated the power of self-sacrifice and the ideological responsibility in thoughts and emotions.

At the time when the termination of the hajj has filled hearts with success and the *ihram, miqat, sa'y*, Arafah, Mash'ar, Mina and stoning *(rami)*, sacrifice and *eid* caused the souls to kindle the fire of faith and love and has made all persons who are shattered in life and torn to pieces by claws and teeth of hundreds of necessities, anxieties and occupations now to be unified in sincerity and complete faith.

In such a land and at such a time—more than a million Muslims throughout the world must not end the hajj without thinking about each other or be dispersed through the earth and creep into the shell of their individual and daily life.

The hajj is to move together from *miqat* to Mina. All three stations of Arafah, Mash'ar and Mina are always there but the hajj does not always exist. It is only now that your breath is filled with the Spirit of God. When tomorrow everyone deserts here, it will become as any corner in the rest of the world and a land with its only characteristic being that it is a place of no water and no life.

You have been brought here to teach you that the seeking of paradise apart from people is an ugly, monk-like selfishness. It is a materialism based on credit which is much worse than a materialism based on cash for it is like a greedy spirit of a business man who has left his seeking after profits, lusts and gluttony to be satisfied after death or is like a stupid bourgeoisie who has refused cash and accepted credit instead.

An ascetic is an egotist just like a materialist. A materialist makes technique into a means and an ascetic, religion. A materialist makes science into a means for seeking pleasure for himself and an ascetic person, God. Both are seeking the same type of paradise. The former looks for it in this world and the latter in another!

But the Islam of Abraham (ع) and Muhammad (ص) has taught us that Allah hates such a holy egotist. If a person neglects serving the people even for a day, does not reflect on the destiny of society and does not even attempt to help, such a person has not only committed a sin but is not even a Muslim.

You have brought the hajj to an end. You have ascended to the highest peak of Abraham's ascension to sacrifice your Ishmael. Yea. But this is not the end of the work. It is the beginning. All of these were to bring you out of serving yourself into serving others.

But not to overlook bread for fame but rather for God. It is thus said, "Come in the season," in order to join with the congregation for if you come late, you are not allowed in the sacred area.

And now, at the end of the hajj, all Abrahams who have destroyed the last base of Iblis—after cutting off the dearest attachments of egotism and after the congregational celebration of victory, O all of you who have succeeded in bringing your 'self' to Mina, before you disperse and even before you go to the House of God, celebrate your two great Abrahamic missions during these two days.

1. Develop an intellectual and scientific conference free for all to participate in.

2. Hold a great social and international congress.

These two days are specific to achieve a result from the hajj, a congress held not in a covered hall but in a mountainous valley, not under a short ceiling but under the high, open sky without doors, walls, restrictions, boundaries or ceremony. A congress held not with the heads of states, official representatives or politicians nor professional diplomats nor political leaders nor secretary generals of political parties nor members of parliament nor senators nor cabinet ministers nor scholars of universities nor religious scholars nor prominent intellectuals nor economic authorities nor social personalities nor official dignitaries. No.

But a congress held from among the people themselves. *"And proclaim the hajj unto the people. They will come to you on foot and on lean camel, coming from every remote way."* (22:27)

Yea. The people themselves! According to Aime Cesaire, "No one has the right to have guardianship of the people or to speak on behalf of the people."

And according to Chandell, "In a place where people are not present, it is a lie to talk about people." It requires a great deal of nerve to do so. Only God has the right to decide on behalf of the people as only the people have the right to be the vice-gerent of God on earth.

It is because of this fact that at the congress of Mina which is held by God, people participate in it without any intermediary.

In this congress, held every year in season, God invites the people of the world so that after the return from the battlefield of Aqabah, the place of sacrifice of Ishmael where they participate and renew their promise to Abraham in the presence of God, to conclude the allegiance made, to attempt to establish faith and the system of monotheism on the earth, to destroy the idols of time, to build the sacred city of the world.

As a body of the followers of the Prophet Muhammad (ﷺ) the Seal of the Abrahamic mission in the history of humanity, he placed the burden of the confirmation of the mission of the Prophets upon the shoulder of the responsible and aware, clear thinkers among the people: the mission to found an *ummah* of witnesses based upon the infrastructure of monotheism, the responsibility to establish wisdom, imamate and equity in the life of humanity and to take over the place of the covenant of God and the people—the land of *jihad*, martyrdom and love—in the name of an *ummah*, committed to the duty of inviting it to beauty and fighting against evil in the life of humanity.

According to the invitation of the Prophet of 'the Book and arms', the front of the hard-liners against the enemy and the soft-liners among themselves in the world should be made clear.

It is in the free congress of Mina where every year all Muslims of the world desert their bloody and duty, closed frontiers and the closed boundaries of political systems because of the invitation of the Lord of the people, the King of the people and the Deity of the people, in order to sit in this open mountainous region under the ceiling of the heavens, freely thinking, discussion problems and finding solutions, seeking help from their fellow companions throughout the world.

And an intellectual and scientific session, not in an amphitheater of an academy nor in scientific gatherings in the universities and not in the surrounding walls specialized for scholars and specialists! A session of a few days, an intellectual and ideological session open to everyone, to scholar and common man, to the professor of the university and the worker of a factory, an eminent and magnificent religious man and an unknown and humble farmer, all have the right to participate, to speak and express an opinion.

Here all signs, grades, colors and distances have been thrown into *miqat*. Here all are one existence: human being. All have one characteristic: haji. And that is all.

There is no higher position for a human being than becoming like Abraham. And here everyone appears in the role of Abraham. Now, at the termination of the hajj, do not disperse, do not return to your country, home, city. You must stay another two days after the *eid* of Sacrifice. Sit. Sit together and meditate together. Give answer to this constant and important question: What should be done in society?

Even before that, sit and meditate in congregation: "What have you done on the hajj?"

CONCLUSION

A GENERAL LOOK

Let us try to reach a conclusion. We should realize what we have done. What meaning did all of this have? What are the secrets?

Sufism, without passing through knowledge (Arafah) and consciousness (Mash'ar) starts from love (Mina) and remains in love (Mina). Philosophy comes as far as consciousness (Mash'ar) but does not reach love (Mina). Civilization, without consciousness (Mash'ar) and love (Mina) stays in knowledge (Arafah). Islam begins from knowledge (Arafah), passes over consciousness (Mash'ar), a dutiful and aggressive passage and then arrives in the phase of ideal and love (Mina)!

And in the land of love, in Mina, how surprising that in this land, there is both God and Iblis!

But here you and your destiny are relevant and not in the world because only God exists in the world, monotheism! Human beings are referred to, in whom reside both the Divine and Iblis. Duality exists in human beings, not in nature. And Mina is the land of your faith and your love, your destiny—where the Divine and Iblis fight inside you for your Ishmael. Mina is the land of your desires.

How amazing! On the day of victory, the *eid* of blood, instead of the celebration of the birth of a child, the celebration of the martyrdom of a child.

The *eid* of sacrifice.

Look to this nation and Tradition, history and glory of these people.

Not the people of blood and dust but the people of ideology and *jihad*!

The *ummah* of monotheism: Servants who carry the mission of freedom of human beings upon their shoulders from the time of Adam till the end of time, who have spread the battle for freedom to the very depths of their primordial nature and who have expanded the scene of the *jihad* from Badr to Mina. The servants who so realize the meaning of freedom that they are bound not only to free themselves from Pharaoh but from Ishmael, as well, and not only from their enemy but from their 'self' as well.

AFTER THE FESTIVAL OF SACRIFICE: STONING THE IDOLS

In the first attack against the last idol, on the first say, you opened the way towards the place of the sacrifice of your Ishmael. You took off the *ihram*, happily celebrated the victory.

And, now, it is the second day. You should stone. You should stone all three idols. This time you should stone in order: first, the first idol, second, the middle idol and third, the last idol.

On the third day, stone all three idols, in sequence, as well. And on the fourth day, you can remain in Mina. And if you stay, you must like two days before, stone all three. And if you go, you must hide your remaining arms in a corner of the battlefield of Mina under the ground.

It is a Command.

After the *eid*, the time of celebration. During the three days after *eid*, you must pause in Mina for stoning.

What does this mean? You may ask yourself:

"On the 10th of Dhihajjah, I achieved the glorious position of Abraham. I found the power to sacrifice Ishmael. In the first attack on the first day, I destroyed Iblis' last base. I made sacrifice. I took off my *ihram*. The victorious battle ended. I celebrated. Then, why again, war after the victory of Mina? Why, then, stoning again after the fall of the last enemy's base?"

This is the lesson. It means that never neglect the dead Iblis who might regain life for a revolution is threatened with destruction, even after victory. It is in constant danger of anti-revolution.

Snakes with smashed heads rise again during the warmth of the glory of victory. The negligence of celebration and the pride of power. They change color: Wear masks of a friend and demolish from inside, usurping all achievements of the revolution. Swallowing that which the *mujahid*s and passion players should inherit from the martyrs. Victory should not lead you to comfort. When you take the reins of Mina in hand, do not let go.

If you throw Iblis out of the door, it will return through the window. If you smash it on the outside, it will grow from the inside. If you weaken it in battle, it will regain power in peace. If you destroy it in Mina, it will destroy you in your 'me'. What am I saying? *Waswasah*, obsessions, have a thousand masks and disguises.

If you uncover the black dress of *kufr*, it puts on the green cloak of religion. If you disgrace it in the visage of *shirk*, it puts on the disguise of *tawhid* If you destroy an idol on its head in the temple, it will make its home in the *mihrab*. If you kill it in Badr, it will take revenge in Karbala. If it is wounded by the sword in Khandaq, it will respond in the Kufa mosque. If you take the idol of Hubal in Uhud, it will raise the Quran of God in its hands in Siffin.

And you, what a simple warrior, thoughtless intellectual! Do you really think that the war has ended on the 10th of Dhihajjah after pounding the enemy's base: that becoming the victor in the battlefield of Aqabah, you take off the battle dress and wear the dress of peace. Apply perfume. Adorn yourself. Celebrate having thought that the *jihad* is over and danger has been uprooted. Do you really think you can leave the scene of Mina? That being saved, you can go to the House of God and occupy yourself with your pilgrimage and worship? Or, as a victor, return to your own home and busy yourself with your daily life?

O Abrahamic *mujahid*! Do not forget that the 10th of Dhihajjah is the *eid* of Sacrifice, not the *eid* of Victory. The sacrifice of Ishmael is not the end of the hajj. It is the beginning. The army of *tawhid* has arrived in the land of love. The ideals of the army of *tawhid* have destroyed the base of the resistance of Iblis and dominate over Mina. O you soldier of *tawhid*! Do not lay down your arms after the victory of the Abrahamic revolution. Do not become intoxicated like victors. The danger of the revival of the defeated enemy still exists. Three bases of Iblis have fallen but they are still erect and have roots in the land of faith.

You should keep up your legendary spirit, state of alertness, *jihad* after victory and the *eid* of Sacrifice. With awareness and precise consciousness of self, with collaboration and coordination, with all the armies who have attacked from Mash'ar and have dominated over Mina, with strategic planning, with the discipline of a pre-determined period, you should continuously and regularly pound the bases of Iblis under a continuing rain of bullets. Uproot them. The revolution is still endangered. The victory of the revolution is also endangered.

Do not become proud in your greatest victory for after becoming Abraham-like, you are still endangered! Even after the sacrifice of your Ishmael, you are endangered! For Iblis is a seven-colored enemy with seventy traps.

Yesterday Iblis made the life of Ishmael a means to deceive you. Today it can make the sacrifice of Ishmael the source of your pride!

Therefore, continuously stone the idols. Pound all these three idols as long as you are in the land of Mina because Mina is the land of your faith and your love, the place of all of your desires and wishes, the front of your victories and glories, the final destination of your migration. It is your hajj and the highest peak of your perfection. It is the ideal of your life and your ideal life.

It is the destination of *tawhid* and more surprising, the place of ambush of your most frightening enemy, the three rebels of *shirk*.

You have faith. Thus you are always in faith and faith is always within you.

Faith is always endangered. And the rebel against God—*taghut*—is always rebellious. After the *eid* of Sacrifice, stone, as well. Stone the three every day as long as you are in Mina.

That is to say, be in *jihad* all your life.

That is say, *jihad* is not the short way to bring you to rulership.

That is to say, *jihad* is not only a means to achieving power.

That is to say, *jihad* does not come to an end after your prevailing over the enemy.

That is to say, celebrate the *eid* of Sacrifice. Do not celebrate the *eid* of victory.

That is to say, take off your *ihram* but do not put down the pebbles.

That is to say, victory can be achieved in a day but if you consider yourself victorious, it will leave all at once.

That is to say, for achieving victory over the enemy, a single stoning but for the destruction of it, even stonings.

The fall of the enemy's base, seven shots. Uprooting it, seventy.

That is to say, divide the arms collected in Mash'ar. How many bullets are they? Seventy? O wonder. Again the number seven, seventy. An attack on the first day to the last idol. For three days after, every day, three attacks, in sequence, to all three idols. In every attack, throw seven stones. Totally seventy. In ten attacks you come to the right figure. But the last three attacks are special to the last day, the 13th of Dhihajjah, the fourth day of the pause. After victory was achieved on the 1st day, the 10th, you are obliged to remain two more days and fight. Continuation of the battle after victory, stoning the three-fold bases, one by one, in sequence.

The fourth day you yourself must choose. You can stay if your duty is not finished in Mina, if you still feel the danger, you can stay and if you stay, you must fight like the two days before. Three attacks in sequence to all three bases. Therefore, you should bring seventy stones from Mash'ar for the battle. That which is a Command, inevitable, is that you should attack three bases seven times. It is because of this that you must divide the arms you collected. One-seventh for achieving victory and six-sevenths of them for the continuation of struggle after victory so that destiny of all movements and the ominous destiny of all revolutions should not be repeated. So that once again the destiny of Islam would not take place in history.

After the victory of Makkah, do not consider the surrender of Abu Sufyan as the Islam of Abu Sufyan. After the victory of the mission, during the twenty-three years of *jihad*, do not consider the fall of *shirk* in the external front, the destruction of the aristocracy in the visage of the idols and the domination of ignorance in the existence of the Quraysh to be victory. You must uproot the three bases of gold, coercion and deception which fell to their knees after Badr, Uhud and Fath during the two centuries and some of imamate with the continuity of *jihad* and the continuation of stoning after the fall of the base of Aqabah so that *shirk* does not wear the dress of *tawhid*. So that satan (*khanas*) who has been defeated at Khandaq does not creep to the opposite side. So that the Age of Ignorance does not become the heir of Islam. If you celebrate victory in Thaqifah, the executioner, in the disguise of the Prophet's caliph will shed in Karbala all that you achieved in Arafah, Mash'ar and Mina and toss it into the Euphrates.

Continue stoning. O Abrahamic *mujahid*! O you who have come from Mash'ar! Iblis awaits in ambush at every one of the three bases in Mina, the land of faith and *jihad*.

As long as you exist, it also exists.

THE LAST MESSAGE OF REVELATION

The hajj, through its movements, declares a message as the Quran does with words. It has been recommended one should read the whole Quran during the hajj. Thus, we must have come to the end of the Quran by now. Now, at the completion of the hajj, let us learn a lesson from the last words of the Holy Book.

The last words of the Quran speak about a danger and the last movements of the hajj speak about stoning.

In the last phase of the hajj, the words are about the stoning of three idols and in the last *surah* of the Quran, negation of three powers. At the completion of the hajj, danger still exists. It addresses the followers of Abraham to fear this danger. At the completion of the Quran, the words refer to an evil and it addresses the Abrahamic Prophet to fear this evil.

Amazing! The Quran has ended and danger has not ended. The victorious mission has ended and danger has still not ended. Prophecy has ended and danger has still not ended.

Amazing! The Quran comes to an end with two *surah*s. The words in both of which speak about taking refuge from evil. In both it is God Who warns. And the person He warns is a person who has completed the mission of monotheism in history, the person who perfected the mission of Abraham. He is Muhammad (ﺹ).

And the hajj comes to an end with a two day pause in both of which stoning is referred to and in both it is God Who warns. The person He warns is the initiator of the mission of monotheism in history.

And you, O follower of the Prophet of Islam. O you who have come to the end of the Tradition of Abraham, not with action but with the secret, where do you go in comfort from Mina?

At the completion of the hajj, O Haj! Let us read to the end of the Quran and see what danger threatens the mission of our victorious Prophet. In addition, before we depart from Mina and leave behind the three destroyed idol bases for our daily life, let us hear the last Message of God as to what danger He warns of to His friend—the human being appointed by Him to the people.

"Say: (O Muhammad): I take refuge
"With the Lord of Daybreak
"From the evil of created things

"And from the evil of the dark night
"When it overspreads
"From the evil of those who practice satanic arts
"From the evil of an envier when he envies." (113:1-5)

Here the words are about the external enemy and external enemies, external to my people, my country and me.

What is objective, what is obvious and what is a face to face war, is the darknesses, decadence and abominations which come like the night over the valley of faith and spread their black tent over it, rush in like a flood, over-flowing into the valley of faith, spreading everywhere and contaminating everything. It also disgraces, abolishes and turns the light of knowledge, the clear sightedness of consciousness and the faith and ideal of love into a swamp. It obliterates and drowns them to such an extent that although you are in faith, you do not see it. Although you are in love, you do not understand it. Although you enjoy love, you do not recognize the Beloved. Although you have faith, you do not find your destination. Although you slaughter your Ishmael, you do not do so at the place of sacrifice of *tawhid* but rather, at the foot of the *taghut*.

The darkness is intolerable.

You stone, but not Iblis, rather angels. You sacrifice, but not a sheep, rather a human being, yourself. You endeavor but not with your feet, rather, under the control of the enemy. You circumambulate but not round the circuit of God, rather with the intention of Nimrod.

Oppression is intolerable.

"When (the dark night) overspreads." (113:3)

And conspiracies both secret and open. Magicians of politics. Enchanters of thought. Blowers of witchcraft. Reciters of deceit who bring dispersion, spread enmity, create rumors, plough seeds of vengeance, change the hands of unity into tight fists to be used against each other. Break ties. Disconnect links. Make brothers enemies and enemies into brothers. Blow the magical spirit into complexes. Disconnect attachments. Paralyze will power. Destroy faith. Slacken decisions. Breach agreements. Turn the unity of religion into group of insects. Cut into pieces the unity of the *ummah* and every sect and every piece a morsel under the claws and teeth of the dark night. For magic blowers are the mercenaries of the dark night as sorcerers work in the shelter of the night and for the night.

And finally, an envious person but not when that person swallows his or her envy, for this is a sick person, a self-tormented sickness, but when he or she envies!

This is no longer the dark night, the foreign oppressor, direct, with coercion, no longer a blower—a hidden and ill-minded agent of the dark night who receives a wage.

But a friend! A sympathizer of the same front. Not an enemy. Not an agent of the enemy. Not an oppressor (*qasit*). Not a plaything of the oppressor, a common fanatic and a holy donkey who misses the truth of religion (*mariqa*) rather, those who break their allegiance (*nakith*)—the dagger-thruster from behind who betrays but who is not considered to be a traitor. Who beats the friend but he is not the enemy. Who is the means of blowers and the pole of the tent of the over-

spreading dark night but wageless and beyond reproach.

He kills but his hands are not polluted with blood.
He commits evil but no one becomes pessimistic about
him. He digs deep wells upon the path of friends, not on
purpose, but rather with a sickness.

The most disgraceful and non-treatable disease: envy.

A complex which destroys a victorious revolution—

And throws down the most courageous *mujahid*s
from the highest peak of glory—

And ritually slaughters friends with the hands of
friends—

And transforms a religious devotee into the lethal
weapons of *kufr* and debauchery—without him wanting it and without the masses knowing it—

And it is therefore possible to rend asunder the tent
of the overspreading dark night over faith,

To excavate the 'den' of the blowers and drive them
from Mina.

"But what do I do with the envious person who is
filled with internal pain?" He is a friend and tool of the
dark night and a plaything of blowers of the dark night.
But like us, he is the enemy of the dark night and
perhaps, more than we, an enemy of the blowers of the
dark night.

And it is because of this that in the rank of these three
evils, the last rank belongs to it.

And on the first day in this Mina, it is the last base
which you should stone.

For it is the final blight of faith and ideals within one.

And here, again the trinity! The three *taghut*s.

The first idol: the dark night, the domination of

night, darkness and oppression.

The second idol: the blower and its agents: sorcerers of dispersion and those who waste thoughts, ethics and awareness, pavers of the way of thoughts and culture for the dark night, hypnotizers of the masses in the skirt of the overspreading night.

The third idol: an envious person. The fifth column of darkness, the unconscious plaything of blowers. A friend in the service of the enemy and with all of this, the saving of love from these three *taghut*s is easier.

Let daybreak appear, the breaker of morning pour a stream of white light over the valley of Mina.

When the blade of the sun tears down the tent of the dark night, it removes the sovereignty of darkness and oppression from Mina, drives blowers who have taken shelter under the dark night to hide under rocks and in the caves of Mina and, finally, when the power of night ceases, the deceit of the sorcerers of the night cease, complexes of envy also remain shut and harmless, buried in the depths of friends!

All these are the work of night. These three evils are the wickednesses of the night. Let the night die. Let the morning dawn rise, O God of dawn!

"Lord of the Daybreak."

But in the last *surah*, the words refer to a most frightening danger. It is however clear that freeing of faith is more difficult.

And it is due to this that Fakhr Razi said about the *surah falaq*, "The stress is on one Quality of God and here (*surah nas*), it is on three Qualities."

From the beginning of the words and the tone of the words, it is clear that the story is very serious, full of conflicts and complicated.

In that *surah*, God is interpreted as the Lord of Daybreak, as the word is about a power—the enemy of daybreak—which lives in darkness. It is sufficient if the dark veil of night is split with a blade of light. When the daybreak appears, they die.

In this *surah*, God is interpreted as Lord, King and Deity of the people. The words refer to powers pretending to be God, the enemies of the people, who are the claimants of three titles of God among the people.

"Say: I take refuge in
"The Lord of the people,
"The King of the people,
"The Deity of the people..." (114:1-3)

In the previous *surah*, the words referred to the world, society and dark powers which dominate over secret agents who intentionally blow evil into thoughts and those selfish persons who, because of sickness, commit treason. The words refer to three anti-human blights, three anti-social powers, three criminal powers: oppression and darkness, corruption and perversion, selfishness and treason. And who are the victims: human beings, human society, the revolutionary movement.

And here it is a social system which is referred to, class infrastructure, people and powers ruling people, those who are involved in the destiny of people, people in their relation to God and to claimants of a deity. Here basic evil and the perpetual enemy of people are referred to, victims, not human kind or human society. Rather a class, 'people'.

It is only in relation to people that an idol is built and

taghut is worshipped, can come to claim God's position, God's Qualities and the title and particularities of God. It is only in relation to God with the people not with the world and nature that it intervenes so that the servants of God are drawn to enslavement and despite the imagination of scholars who think in solitude—who read facts in textbooks not in the context of realities—*tawhid* and *shirk* are not just two philosophical views—theological discussions within the four walls of schools and temples.

But rather they are living realities, in the depths of the human being's primordial nature, in the context of the life of the masses, in the heart of encounters, contradictions, the movement of history, the class war of people and enemies of people throughout time, opposed to what those thinkers who think in solitude imagine, *shirk* is a religion, a religion ruling over history. Yea, the opium of the people! And *tawhid* becomes the condemned religion of history, the blood of people. The primordial nature, mission, weapon of the people and the greatest and most profound, most clandestine tragedy of humanity—so much so that intellectuals have still not discovered it—is the enslavement of people with the sole claim of freedom of the people. The death and abjectness of the people with the capital resources of life and the honor of the people! How? By metamorphosizing religion through religion! The great hypocrisy of history. Iblis in the sacred image of God! *Tawhid* in the service of *shirk*! *Shirk*? Religion in the hands of earthly gods, the signs of satan! *Khanas*! *Khanas*— the greatest evil and enemy of the people, *nas*.

And it is because of this that the word *nas* , people, is

repeated everywhere.

Who are these gods of the earth who have established powers for themselves among the people? Who are these *taghuts* who have rebelled against God and the people and have revolted against the Truth?

Again, three *taghuts*! Trinity!

Usurper of these three titles, declared in this *surah* for God and a particularity of God alone.

Tawhid the unity of Qualities!

And its opposite, *shirk*, trinity of *shirk*, Cain, the executioner who appears in three visages and reigns over the people—children of the martyred Abel.

Cain is one. Pharaoh, Karun and Balam b. Ba'ur are three manifestations of this one, not three bodies, but three visages.

And strangely enough, all trinities of history are like this. In all religions of three gods, the deity is one with three faces.

At the beginning, humanity lived as brothers because forests and streams were the property of all peoples. They all ate freely of the blessings of nature as God was the Owner and all servants were equal, the age of freely hunting and fishing. Anyone who caught a wild beast, tamed it. Ethics were Abelian. Cain became a farmer, saying: This land is my property. That is, does not belong to you.

It is one, but, at the same time, three. It is three and, at the same time, one!

Oneness was changed to two and the worship of One was changed to the worship of two. Cain took the place of God, appearing in three visages and the worship of three, trinity!

Trinity, this disgraceful triangle in which all Prophets, longers for justice and martyrs of humanity are buried.

A disgraceful talisman, which, like the yoke of captivity, fell upon the neck of the people making servants of the Lord of the universe, the slaves of the gods of society, a triangular talisman! Three partners of one company! The first one enchained the necks of the people. The second one emptied their pockets and the third—partner of the other two—in the disguise of a spiritual man, in the language of the heavens, hummed in their ears: "Have patience, my religious brother. Leave the world to those who are of it. Let hunger be the capital for the pardon of your sins. Forebear the hell of life for the rewards of paradise in the Hereafter. If they only knew the reward of people who tolerate oppression and poverty in this world, they would begrudge you your future prosperity, even though you be the misfortune of today. Keep your stomach empty of food, O brother, in order to see the light of wisdom in it.

"What is the remedy? Whatever befalls us. The pen of destiny has written on our foreheads from before: The prosperous are prosperous from their mother's womb and the wretched are wretched from their mother's womb.

"Every protest is a protest against the Will of God. Give thanks for His giving or non-giving. Let the deeds of everyone be accounted for on the Day of Reckoning. Be patient with oppression and give thanks for poverty. Do not breathe a word so that you do not lose the reward of the patient in the Hereafter. Release your body so as not to require clothes! Do not forget that the protest of a creature is protest against the Creator.

"The accounting of Truth and justice is the work of God, not the masses. In death, not in life. Do not pass judgment for the Judge of the judgment is God. Do not be shamed on the Day of Resurrection when you see that God, the Merciful, the Compassionate forgives the oppressor who you had not forgiven in this world. Everyone is responsible for his own deeds. The command to good and preventing evil? Yea. But first: its condition is having knowledge and piety. Second: having certainty that it will have an effect and will result in a change and thirdly: if there is the possibility of there being a loss or harm for you, the duty is cancelled."

And these three are accomplices and collaborators. Cain in three masks, the three constant gods of the trinity, whether in the dress of *kufr* or Islam, *shirk* or *tawhid* , ruling over the destiny of the masses, always and everywhere—in the name of religion—over the expanse of the earth throughout time!

These three *taghut*s are three visages of Cain: Cain the owner who murdered his brother Abel, the shepherd and then his children, without a father, in the guardianship of their uncle, the murderer.

An executioner, the heir of the one he martyred.

Wonder! That the Abrahamic Prophets—callers to the One God and justice, heirs to Abel, human beings in the age of pastoralism and equality—were all shepherds.

According to the explicit declaration of the last messenger of these appointed shepherds, the "Prophet of the people" appointed by God, the Prophet who himself grazed the sheep of the people of Makkah in Qararit—

"There is no Prophet who did not graze sheep!" There is no bearer of a mission who did not graze sheep.

And this is the tradition of Cain and his triple sons: wolf, fox and rat and their perpetual struggle in history to nurture lambs, the children of Abel—the people—through despotism, deception or exploitation.

And, therefore, we see that in every age, instead of a philosopher, scholar, wise man and leader, in a civilized town, in the heart of a culture, a traditional center of learning or a religious temple, a shepherd from among the people arose suddenly, with an astonishing rage, from the bosom of the dry desert and released the sheep, attacked the gods of the earth with his shepherd's staff in order to guide and bring salvation for the *ummah* which was being slaughtered by Cainian powers!

It is here one realizes the profound meaning and beauty of the Words of God in the Quran Who repeats: "A Messenger is sent from the people themselves. He is sent with the language people speak." It explicitly says, *"We sent Messengers with distinct signs and with them We revealed the Book and Balance so people would revolt for equality and justice and also iron descended with them which carries strength and profit for the people."*

And it is because of this that throughout history, wherever a Prophet was appointed by God from among the people themselves or a longer for justice arose from among the people with the responsibility of calling the children of Abel—the people—to monotheism, justice and consciousness, they attacked him with full force and killed him. And then after a full generation or less, they would take on the role of mourners of him, heirs to his faith and custodians of his *ummah*.

If a Prophet was victorious over them, they submitted themselves, changed their clothes and in a full generation or less became his Caliph and deputy, master of his banner, Book seal and sword!

There is one Cain and in three visages. Or seven colors and seventy disguises, seven thousand names, seventy thousand traps. There is one Cain who is a murderer and his brother, his victim. There is one Cain who is a possessor and people are his possession. There is one Cain who is ruler and people are his condemned. There is one Cain who is a witch and people are his bewitched. And it is ownership which made two brothers, enemies. Two equalities into two inequalities. Human beings into two races, society into two classes, history into two dimensions, one God into two gods: duality.

According to the Quran: arrogance and deprivation!

What is deprivation? What a great and 'roomy' word. Anything that deprives people and drives them to being deprived. There is one Cain and one deprivation in three dimensions from three bases at the hands of his three sons: either put him in chains with force: despotism, politics, Pharaoh!

Or suck his blood through gold: exploitation, economy, Karun!

Or deceive him with hypocrisy: deception, faith, Balam b. Ba'ur.

And there is one ruling class in three visages. There are three ruling powers in one class. There is one Cain who finds three manifestations and changes one god into three: trinity!

One, and, at the same time, three: three and, at the

same time, one!

But in seven colors, seventy disguises, seven hundred names, seventy thousand traps!

Wearing a disguise or undisguised. *Kufr* or religion. *Shirk* or *tawhid*. Whip or law. Dictatorship or democracy. Enslavement or liberty. Feudalism or bourgeoisie. Religion or science. Spirituality or intellectualism. Philosophy or Sufism. Pleasure or asceticism. Savageness or civilization. Decadence or progress. Materialism or spiritualism. Christianity or Islam. Sunni or Shi'ite.

They come and go. If you drive them away from the door, they return over the wall. If you crush slavery, the master becomes a feudalist and the slave, a peasant. If you destroy feudalism through great revolutions, the feudalist becomes a capitalist and the former is made into a worker.

Moses drowns Pharaoh in the waters of the Nile with the miraculous power of the whitened hand of monotheism, buries Karun in the earth and effaces the religion of witchcraft with the staff of the mission.

But the Pharaoh drowned in the Nile immediately raises his head out of the River Jordan and becomes the heir of Moses in the name of Shamoon, takes the staff of Moses in hand instead of the whip. The sorcerers of Pharaoh become the sons of Aaron and companions of Moses, taking in hand the Pentateuch, instead of the magic staff. Balam b. Ba'ur becomes the Sign of God. Karun receives the trust of monotheistic people; and all three swallow up Palestine in the name of the Promised Land: the Septians of old build the new Coptics!

The promised Christ appears and abolishes the Jewish religion, stones the Roman Empire. Caesar becomes

Pope. Jewish rabbis become Christian monks. The Jewish rabbis become priests. Roman senators become cardinals of the Vatican. The palace becomes a church. Caesar becomes Pope and Jupiter becomes Christ.

Muhammad (ﺹ) arises. Caesar and Khosroe are stoned. Priest and high priest are rejected. Arab and non-Arab aristocrats are negated. Caesar and Khosroe become Caliph. Priest and high priest: religious leader and judge. Landlords, commanders, dignitaries, aristocratic families, feudalists and nobles become companions, masters, holy personalities and owners possessing noble descent and lineage. The Sassanid monarchy and the Roman empire become the caliphate of God's Prophet in name. Churches and fire temples become mosques. Massacres become *jihad*. Plunderings become the poor-rate (*zakat*). The abjectness of the people becomes the Will of God.

The family of Muhammad (ﺹ) is either killed or imprisoned. It becomes the victim of usurpation, oppression, massacre and captivity while the family of Abu Sufyan and Abbas become heir to Muhammad (ﺹ).

Ali (ﻉ) in opposition, stands firm for the continuation of the Prophet's Tradition. True leaders fight against the caliphate for 250 years and become martyrs. Carrying the banner of true leadership during the reign of oppression, their justice-seeking followers continue the red course of Shi'ism. In order to abolish oppressive regimes and unjust commands, they make imamate and justice the slogans of their religion during the rule of the Traditions of ignorance and reigns of the aristocratic caliphate.

After the elapse of a thousand years of *jihad* and martyrdom upon the way of imamate and justice, suddenly the caliph becomes a Shi'ite. The Safavid monarchy becomes heir to the Alavi leadership. The house of the caliphate becomes the palace of the High Gate (*aliqapu*).

In Europe, the Renaissance gains victory over the church. Science replaces religion. Old schools become abandoned in the face of newly established universities and scholars drive clergymen to the corners of temples. Balam b. Ba'ur comes from the church to the university.

The revolution in France uproots feudalism. Karun, the landlord, is stoned in the countryside. He immediately returns to town and becomes a banker.

Pharaoh's head is cut by the blade of the guillotine of the revolution. He is stoned out of the palace of Versailles but with the treasure of Karun and the witchcraft of Balam, he pops his head out of the democratic ballot box.

Our cousins do not leave us alone, that is, the three sons of Cain. The same three brothers who are accomplices and collaborators in all times and in all places. If you take the whip of coercion away from the wolf, the rat will buy you with gold. If you do not sell out, the fox will deceive you with religion. And if that does not work, with science. And if that does not work, with philosophy. And if that does not work, with ideology. If that does not work, with games. If that does not work, with futile struggle or with sham fights. If that does not work, with weeping and lamentation, prayer, mourning, beating your chest and head, uproar, subjectivity, spiritual amusements, whatever makes you neglect the present. All hates are made to face towards history. All loves belong to after death!

And if that does not work, it will deceive you with the insanity of consumption, pleasures, luxury, pretense, grade, cash on hand, loan, installments, working like a dog and its name, life. Work and overtime wages and its name, welfare! Fright, flattery and abjectness, spending life running from morning to night and standing in the back rows for a few years! All freedoms, values and opportunities are sacrificed for luxury. Offering your future to the new masters for what you ate in the past. Selling the comforts of life in order to purchase the means of comfort, galloping till death and during a lifetime, not having a moment for deliberation, not finding a chance for understanding. If that does not work, the commotion of jazz, sex and... and if that does not work, the allures of Sufism, the ecstasy of heroin, marijuana, LSD and thousands of other techniques and thousands of other so-called truths and falsehoods, whatever will keep you occupied with yourself and heedless of them!

Whatever stops you from the way, whether it be called*kufr* or faith.

And we people, the deprived everywhere upon the earth, the continuous minor orphans of all ages, the true servants of God, the real children of Adam, the sentries of brotherhood, the true lovers of equality, the representatives of pure primordial nature (*fitrah*) the rightful *tawhid* unity, peace...the remains of an age in which humanity was a unified *ummah* at the table of the Lord of nature. All these blessings were buried under the earth with the martyrdom of Abel, when the blood of our father—the innocent victim of ownership—was spread over the earth through deceit and treachery and they remained within us as desire, faith.

And with his vengeance, the restlessness of a mission, which exists within us as the flame of hope.

The banner of *tawhid*, the belief in the One God, is the torch of this hope and the knowledge of this mission which is passed from hand to hand by the appointed shepherds, messengers from the history of knowledge (Arafah) to faith (Mina), becomes the heritage of generation after generation from Abel to Abraham, from Abraham to Muhamamd (ﷺ), from Muhammad to Husayn (ع) and from Husayn. (ع): In every month, in every day, in every land, until the end of time, until the world-wide revolution for justice under the leadership of the deprived of history for this is the inheritance of the deprived upon the earth.

Switching hands, the banner draws a red line on the surface of the earth and on the bed of history.

And the banner of *shirk*—the belief in multiple gods—is the banner of tyranny, hunger and ignorance and it stands hoisted in the hands of the three satans.

Kufr and religion are not prejudice and schism, are not non-afflicted visions of an non-afflicted philosopher or Sufi. *Kufr* and religion are the depravity and growth of humanity.

The qualities of *kufr* and religion are clear and the signs of each are apparent. We are talking about growth and depravity and the war between equity and cruelty. If anything but these elements exists, they are deceit and hypocrisy. Do not listen to just any words because in this totally hypocritical history, only the children of

Cain have the right to speak or even talk about right and religion. What am I saying? Only they have the right to speak about the martyred Abel and the destiny of Abel's survivors.

Listen to the words of the Quran alone and not to those who speak for it as Cainians have also become commentators. Listen only to the Quran. It is the only document preserved from their theft. Listen to it to tell of the history of mankind and interpret the meaning of mission.

"People were but one ummah." (2:213)

The people were a unique society. God appointed the Prophets, those warners and bringers of good tidings, those makers of disputes not because of prejudice, not because of diversity of opinions and faith, not unconsciously but consciously because of evil intentions and envy, to disregard rights and oppression.

Listen to the words of God to tell you what the Prophets were assigned to do and why they have been sent to us. *"Indeed We sent Our Messengers with the clear signs and We sent down with them the Book and the Balance so that people arise for equity."* (57:25)

Equity means: the realization of this principle: Everyone according to his share and right. And now, growth and depravity have been separated and the boundary of each made clear, the boundary of *kufr* and religion are evident, the roles of each are clear.

Kufr and religion, *shirk* and *tawhid* stand opposite each other with clear and distinguishable ranks.

Refer again to the Quran to show you simply, straightforwardly, clearly and effectively but not in sophisticated words of philosophy and Sufism, nor scholarly words but in words the common people may understand and better understand, decisive and clear.

"The believers fight in the Way of God and the kafir fight in the way of the taghut." (4:76) and immediately issues the command, "Fight you, therefore, against the friends of satan, for the trick of satan is weak."

Who are its friends?

Yea. The three-fold *taghut*.

And you, Companions of God! O you in restless offensive against Iblis! Wearing the dress of piety, protect your Divine self in the highest tower of wisdom from the poisonous, black winds of witchcraft.

The spider of deception has woven a web of oppression from the warp of wealth and the weft of coercion upon the Way of God. "Do not fear death. Do not ask for reprieve for a murderer. Exercise piety. You will not be oppressed, even to the extent of a tiny white fissure in the groove of a date seed."

And you, monotheistic human being who is responsible for the reprisal of Abel, who carry on your shoulders the mission of all Messengers of the Book, Balance and Iron.

O heir of Adam! People!

O symbol of power, freedom and consciousness! Seek refuge in the One God from these *taghuts* who deprive through *shirk* because He is the

Lord of the people.

King of the people.

Deity of the people.

You who have passed through Arafah, Mash'ar and Mina upon the red line of martyrdom, and have stepped on the ruins of the *taghut* of Aqabah—

And you who have ascended monotheism's highest peak of freedom, you have conquered Mina's land your self.

O follower of Abraham's mission! O follower of the Prophet's Tradition!

Be aware. Fear!

You are endangered!

In danger of Cain, in danger of the return of the three Cainian *taghut*s.

The Prophet is endangered because the message of the Prophet is endangered.

The *ummah*, followers of the Prophet, are endangered, that is, you are endangered.

Your liberty, your life and your faith. Monotheism is endangered.

Fear.

Fear the evil of the three *taghut*s.

Take refuge in the Lord, Master and Deity of the people.

There are three *taghut*s and one Iblis, one Cain. Fear "from the evil of the slinking whisperers" which brings harm to the intellect for it is the return of clandestine deceit. Who "whispers in the breasts of people," tempts the inner nature of unconscious people "from among jinn and people." Who is a *waswas*? What is it?

Dictionaries give its meaning as: tempters and also a disease which appears after the prevalence of melancholy and destroys the mind. Melancholy. As well as evil deeds. Malicious thinking or absurdity or emptiness which penetrates into the soul of the human being and then is blown into the unconsciousness of people.

Whatever inspires you, falls into your unconsciousness, comes to you, talks to you, unheard by your ears, unseen by your eyes.

What is this *waswas*, this melancholy, the tempter which brings harm to the mind and damages consciousness of self?

It is *khanas*.

What is *khanas*.

Dictionaries define it: Any element which diverts you, attaches you to itself, causes you to vanish, covers and conceals you in itself, keeps you within itself, imprisons you, pursues you like an eagle which pursues its prey. It is hidden, a concealer, a tricky and deceitful element which is after you, always playing tricks on you. It has continuous deceitful contacts with you. It does not leave you alone. It comes and goes. If you expel it, it returns again. What does this satanic temptation do? It projects *waswasah*.

What is *waswasah*?

Dictionaries define it as: the element which contaminates you with evil or emptiness, which carries neither profit nor value, neither benefit nor blessing. It is solely only absurdity, emptiness, whatever brings harm to the intellect of the human being and leads that person into delirium, makes a person speak incoherently, senselessly. It strikes one dumb, metamorphosized and alien to the self in one's human soul.

What is the quality of this tempter? Who is this satan which brings temptation? It is both of *jinn* and human being. *Jinn*? An invisible creature. An unseen, hidden power. A power which penetrates, penetrates into humanity but is neither human nor visible.

Alas! How true it is and how clear! And today, more

clear than any previous time, more harsh than ever, tragic.

Those three *taghut*s are hidden and manifest. They leave, change color and return. They are defeated, yet raise their heads again.

Today in the capitalistic and machine-age system, where neo-colonialism dominates through hidden colonialism, in the conspiracy of the metamorphization of cultural colonialism, sickened by the colonial-toxication, advanced techniques and brain washing, those three *taghut*s more tragically than ever are occupied with metamorphosizing the human being.

Look at what Chandell says: "The great tragedy for the human being of today is not the explosion of the atomic bomb but rather the transfiguration and metamorphosis of human essence. Claiming the humanness of the human species! They are, with great speed, creating a new type of phenomenon which is no longer a human being, but rather, a pseudo-human machine which neither God nor nature created...it is a slave who does not know its master, does not see him, is free and strives only to become a slave. He can be bought with gold but he pays the price himself. He waits in a long line beside the thief's house until the turn of plundering him comes for he undertook great efforts to be in this line! He will no longer grow. He will be moulded. He can now have everything but in return for that, he loses everything. He only believes in the melancholic religion. In this state of melancholia, that which he pays is always more costly than what is given in return. Before his birth, he had been determined. He does not live, rather, he is installed. He has found the chance to gallop until the end of the universe but he loses God and humanness forever."

A more frightening tragedy than can be imagined.

The genus of primordial nature is being transfigured.

Those three *taghut*s no longer tempt with just force of blade, power of gold and deceit of the *tasbih*. Today, coercion and gold have employed the extraordinary, deceitfulness, darkening and destructive power of science, the astonishing magic of art and the gigantic power of technique, as well.

Today necks are being freed from enchainment but the people of the world are being internally enchained. They are free to place a vote in a box, in favor of whoever they like, but the satan of *jinn* and men had previously cast the vote in their hearts.

The tragedy of today is alienation. What does it mean to be alienated? An alienated person is a person whose human essence, whose true character and whose consciousness of self have been covered over and sit in place of self, whose intellect has been harmed. Political dictatorship, social discrimination, the savage exploitation of the ancient West have been driven away but all have returned more harsh than before in the shape of the capitalist system, hiding itself under the disguise of liberalism and democracy.

Slavery, serfdom and savage plunders of the Mongols and Ghengis Khan, enslavement of nations by the savage, ancient regimes of the Timurid and Il-Khanid times have been derived from the East. Yet all have returned more metamorphosized and destructive than before in the form of colonialism, hidden in the disguise of modernization and civilization. Military executioners, hired professional assassins of the old colonialism have moved away from the Third World and have returned in the name of economic order, political regime, social relationships, the philosophy of education and training, culture, art, ethics, freedom of sex, the ideology of emptiness and absurdity, the blowing of witchcraft, propaganda, incantation of the blowers of the press, obsession with literature, art and mode...in dutiful treatises, traditional relationships, attachments of faith and the melancholy of nihilism, insanity of culture-toxication, the worship of consumption, worship of sex and the worship of the West...in the invisible dress of neo-colonialism, appearing not in military bases, behind desks, in the streets and bazaar, in the form of human beings but in hidden and unseen hands, invisible powers and relationships in the foundation of economics, the social order, in the depth of thought, ideology, institutions, symbols and styles, the social relationships, spirit, emotion and ethics, value, vote and human intellect which have infiltrated like jinn.

During these fourteen centuries there has been no era which could interpret these miraculous verses as our era can. Throughout five hundred centuries of mankind's fate on earth, never before has the *khanas* made the human being its hidden and manifest victims as in our era. Never before have such temptations, consciously or unconsciously, drawn the hearts of people to destruction.

Yea. Never have these last miraculous, eloquent verses of revelation been so explicitly exegized! The intellectual of today who knows this century, the conscious sociologist of today who knows capitalism and neo-colonialism can clearly see: how, for the sake of a handkerchief of the Caesar, a fire is lit in the palace. How, with the miracle of science, counterfeit is made. How, in the name of civilization, ignorance is created. How satanic tempters and magic blowers deprive people of their culture, faith, consciousness and empty them of their free will from within—make them absurd. Empty of the human being of the 'self' and alienated with the self so humanity will become the tools of imitation and people simply the mouth of consumption and nothing more.

The conscious humanist of today who is not enclosed in the narrow moulds of tribe and traditions, who is not preoccupied in local problems and historical prejudices or the straightened circumstances of guilds, training and heritage, whose glance does not slide solely on the surface of political events, is not busied with temporary appearances, making simple and quick evaluations of daily phenomena, evident relationships, pleased with simple solutions, rather, under all that occurs in the layers of this age, sees the human being and realizes what goes on inside. He can understand that the colonialism of nations, capitalism, class exploitation, the igniting of war, massacres of millions and millions, economic colonialism, plundering material resources and natural resources of the world of the poor, plunderings and plunderings, domination of executionist elements over the destiny of nations, abolishment of human rights...

All, yea. But these are all external tragedies. Political, military, economic, national, legal tragedies...the most frightening tragedy is the tragedy of humanity, the tragedy which penetrates the inner being of people. Those tragedies are ones mentioned in the Quran in the previous verse, the governing evil of the dark night, the evil of blowers, the evil of those who are evil, psychotic, treacherous elements and it is because of this that they are regarded as unimportant. The most dreadful tragedy is the tragedy which threatens the species of humanity and the natural substance of people of the world with metamorphization, the tragedy of the alienation of a person's essence. It is the tragedy of changing a human being to other than a human being. It is the tragedy of temptation! Temptations like those three evils do not harm the existence of human beings. It is the essence of the human being which is thereby wounded. It is because of this tragedy that the wounded and aware conscience of the real intellectual today moans and cries out.

Yea. It is he who sees who the satans of the people are. It is he who realizes who those satans' jinn are because it is he alone who knows the meaning of temptation and feels the extent and depth of the tragedy of the temptation of the life of the human being, he turns away from the killing of human rights for the truth of the human being is also killed.

It is he who knows that the satan—the constant idol-carver, everywhere and in every place, is not a human factor. Sometimes it is a devil and sometimes it is a mysterious power. Sometimes it is covered and hidden. It does not always place the bridle of captivity around the necks. It tempts from inside. Quietly, covered, it steps inside the human being. It infiltrates your essence, your personality, your humanness, your 'you-ness', penetrates and sits instead of your 'self'. It makes you insane. It harms your intellect. It jinn-toxicates you, alienates you.

Yea. A danger more frightening than ever lies in ambush for you, not only in the ambush of mountains or behind rocks but in the ambush of your heart, in your chest, behind the layers of your mind, not only in ambush for your life, your property, but in ambush for your humanness, in ambush for your faith, your *ummah*, your understanding, your consciousness, your love, your victory, the achievements of your *jihad*, the *jihad* of your generation, the heritage of your history, upon the course of your becoming Abraham, in the migration of your becoming Divine-like.

Your enemy is not always armed or an army. It is not always eternal, not always apparent. Sometimes it is a system. Sometimes it is an emotion. Sometimes it is a thought. Sometimes it is a possession. Sometimes it is a method of life. Sometimes it is a method of work. Sometimes it is a way of thinking. Sometimes it is a tool of work. Sometimes it is in the form of productivity. Sometimes it is a kind of consumption. Sometimes it is a culture of life. Sometimes it is cultural colonialism, religious deception. Sometimes it is class exploitation. Sometimes it is the mass media. Sometimes it is the invisible propaganda of a spider-like network. Sometimes it is the world of a new life. Sometimes it is bureaucracy, technocracy and automation; sometimes it is chauvinism, nationalism or racism; sometimes it is the egotism of Nazism, the gold diggers of the bourgeoisie or militarism's love of coercion; sometimes it is the worship of pleasure, of epicureanism; sometimes it is the worship of a subjective idealism or the worship of the objective of materialism or the worship of beauty of art, the worship of sentiments of romanticism, the tendency towards absurd existentialism; sometimes it is the Sufic worship of the spirit; the monk-like worship of asceticism; the racist worship of earth and lineage; the fascist worship of heroes and governments; individualism's worship of the individual; socialism's worship of the collective; communism's worship of economics; philosophy's worship of the intellect; gnosis' worship of feelings; spirituality's worship of heaven; materialism's worship of the world; idealism's worship of imaginings; realism's worship of what exists; the pre-destination of fate's worship of the law; the pre-determinism of destiny's will. Sometimes it is Freudism's love of sex; sometimes epicurean's love of the stomach; sometimes biology's worship of instincts; sometimes *kufr*'s love of this world; sometimes religious worship of science!

These are the idols of the new multitheism: Lat, Uzza, Isaf and Na'ilah of the new Quraysh, three hundred and sixty idols, the Ka'bah of this civilization!

It is here that you realize what the worship of God is.

How broad is the meaning and greatness of the mission of monotheism!

You see that the human being today who says he has switched from devotion to reason and has freed self from religion with the power of science and human liberty not only does not worship God but he has only destroyed monotheism, not worship and servitude. The new multitheism has greater numbers as well as inferior gods in comparison to the old multitheism during the time of the Age of Ignorance. At the time of the Age of Ignorance, savage Arabs worshipped artistic and beautiful statues studded with gems, built of gold or red rubies. It was the manifestation of power, beauty, perfection, blessing and welfare. It was the god of art, the powers of nature, angels, lords and fictitious personalities but from the beyond and sacred. And today, the beloved of the religion of the new multitheism has decreased to the lowest of the low of the genital organ, the most inferior organ of the human body.

Thus the constant *taghut*s who exist everywhere today create injustices more than ever and every place the Pharaoh of today is a system. The Karun of today is a class and Balam b. Ba'ur has taken off the clothes of religion and put on the clothes of science, ideology and art.

How amazing! In the next to the last surah, the Quran speaks of three evils but stresses the One Quality of God, the daybreak!

And in the last surah it speaks about one evil and three Qualities: Lord, King and Deity.

Those three evils are external tragedies of anti-human powers which disregard his rights. And this one evil is an internal tragedy which kills the truth. The sovereignty of the dark night, the thought-destroying blowers and the losses of traitors who blow, kill, plunder and trample upon human rights and human liberties, who nourish people's poverty, captivity and ignorance, however, at any rate, the human being remains under the destruction of these tragedies. But the real tragedy is this that these anti-human powers today, more than ever before, empty the human being from the inside and paralyze his human values in order to dominate, plunder and exploit. Because the experience of history has taught the triple powers that in order to economically and politically enslave a class, nation, and people, one must, at the beginning, put a person into human captivity and silencing that person from within, make the institutions of a person's primordial nature, sick, metamorphosized. This is the evil which is more frightening than the other three evils. Even though evil forces are the same every place, but in the system of the triple rule, the harm which is caused to the human primordial nature of a human being, a tragedy which causes fear in the conscious conscience of a human being today, is that very satan (*khanas*), the enemy of the people who comes and goes every place in three visages and every time in a different disguise.

Temptation is a people-killing tragedy and a position which this three-headed, one hundred visaged snake injects into the human being. Was it not that Iblis, in the disguise of a snake, deceived Adam and caused him to be expelled from God's paradise?

The evil of *waswasah*, temptation, is born of those three evils, the omnious performer of the *taghut* is *khanas*. The Quran teaches us in its last message that the evil which is much more tragic than the other three evils is the temptations of satan (*waswasah-i-khanas*) itself which are a tragedy caused by those three *taghut*s of multitheism and that these temptations are more wicked and lethal than that of those three *taghut*s of multitheism. In order to destroy these three-fold powers which take the human being into captivity, plunder and perversion, only

Divine-like consciousness of self is sufficient; the night must be split by the blade of daybreak. But for the Iblis-like power of satan which infiltrates into the essence of people and turns them; into the tempted *waswas*, one must take refuge in monotheism. It is with the unity of the three powers of Lordship, Kingship and Divinity in the Essence of God alone that one can uproot the foundation of the trinity in human nature and human society as well. One can then lay the foundation for an Abelian society based upon social and human unity built from a unique monotheistic soul in the world view of monotheism. It is then that the model *ummah* should be developed, an *ummah* which invites, knowing Abraham's mission and the sealing of it. The responsibility for its foundation is laid upon the shoulders of the people.

Today people have felt the tragedy. We who are the heirs of Abraham in the world should teach the conscious, struggling and justice-seeking generation of today the mission of salvation of the people of the world which stands on the verge of final extinction. The Quran, the family of Ali and the hajj have made our responsibility extremely heavy.

The dark night, now, more overspread, rules everywhere in the world; magician blowers exist who are more powerful and more concealed than at any time before. Everywhere the sovereignty of the human being over the self is today weaker than in all other eras. The temptations of satan—either from jinn or men—are stronger and more tragic today.

O who stand in the Station of Abraham and upon whose shoulders the seal of revelation has placed the heavy duty of the mission upon your shoulders!

O conscious human being! Vice-gerent of God! Heir to the Prophets! O who must adopt the Prophet as a symbol for yourself so that people can adopt you as their own symbol! O responsible for building the *ummah*, followers of the religion of the Book, scale and iron!

O arisen for equity upon the earth! O enemy of the tyrant, friend of the oppressed! O Muslim *mujahid*!

Respond to the call of the deprived of the earth who are the leaders of the time, heirs of the world and tomorrow's history for the world has been filled with the tyranny of Sufyani tyrants, with the oppression of the Karun-like hoarders of wealth, with the appearance of a blind-folded conspiracy of a one-eyed anti-Savior and the arising for the promised salvation, revenger, Truth, justice and peace at the end of time has begun to show its signs in the depths of the conscience of the anguished masses and responsible intellectuals.

O he who has developed his Divine-like self himself! Heir of the Prophets, superior to the Prophets of the Israelite tribes! Muhammad-like individual who must bear witness to the Truth of time and must be the symbol of the masses of the world, a righteous servant of God who must be Divine-like in this nature! O born of up-righteousness who returns from the circumambulation of love, the search for water, the stations of awareness, consciousness and love, the stoning of the trinity of multitheism, and the sacrifice of Ishmael, carrying the salvation bearing banner of the monotheism of Abraham, the message of the Quran and the sword—Dhulfaqar— of Ali and who has brought as a gift, a pitcher of water from Zamzam as a gift, before you return to your home and begin your daily life, stop for a moment and think about your faith, your covenant. Take a look at yourself, your age, your generation, the countenance of the earth and the face of your contemporary human being. Listen to the cry of the awakened consciences of the world, how they mourn from the evil of satan's temptations.

Toynbee sees human civilization threatened by an internal enemy, the mad and unaccountable rush for consumption, consumption and consumption.

Marcuse has warned that the human being has become one-dimensional like a tool

Eric Fromm, Diogenes-like searches hopelessly around this town with an extinguished light for an aware human being. Camus cries out, "The plague has spread into the town of Oran, the civilized city-state of its age, and innocent children have died in the temple of this city from a mysterious, frightening disease without even knowing why." Jean Isoleh speaks about an armed prince who is fully prepared and decorated with gold but suffers from an intolerable and mysterious disease which has no medical cure!

The conscious carvers of Holland have created the figure of a man in the center of the newly built town of Rotterdam which has firmness of stone but its joints are so separated that it is as if it were about to fall.

Eliot and Joyce have taken a Greek goddess from mythology, the goddess being hermaphrodite, neither man nor woman, and have created it as the god of today's humanity.

And Eugene Ionesco shows the human tragedy in whom satan has infiltrated and turned into a rhinoceros.

Kafka has illustrated the horrible and pitiful portrait of a human being who was supposed to be the representative of God in nature and who God created similar to His Divinity and has revealed how he has been metamorphosized.

Yea. The image of Dorian Grey is not the image of Oscar Wilde. It is the image of the alienated human being of today.

Escape at daybreak, you conscious victim of tragedy! As the dark night overspreads everywhere, artful enchanters blow in difficulties.

So those with complexes of envy have become playthings of night magicians and friends with enmity inside.

Take refuge in the Lord of the Daybreak.

For it splits the nape of night and lets flow the white stream of morning over this love, this faith.

Fear.

Those three *taghut*s have returned, wearing disguises, well-skilled and with an endless army; and hidden weapon. O avenger of the blood of your father! Heir of Abel!

Cain has not died.

Heir of Adam! Before whom the angels prostrated themselves.

Iblis will take revenge. Keep away from this three-faced tempter of seventy colors and seventy thousand traps who protects temptation.

Who whispers inside the masses.

Be alert! Take refuge in God—Muhammad-like—in the Lord of Daybreak, Lord of the people, King of the people, Beloved of the people, and you, O pilgrim!

After the Festival

Stay in Mina.

Everyday regularly stone the three *taghu*ts in sequence, seven times and each time, seven stones. Every day is a *tashrigh*, every month, Dhihajjah, ever land is Mina and human being, history and ....

Life is the hajj.

A FINAL WORD

Now the pause in Mina has ended. The hajj has been completed behind the walls of Makkah. You have another circumambulation and endeavor left (*tawaf al-nisa*). It is said that you can perform this until the end of Dhihajjah, whenever you desire and, even if necessary, perform it before Arafah!

Thus, the hajj has ended. The hajj was all of this. Now, O you who leave Mina, you have passed the last phase of the hajj.

And you have disconnected your futile and repetitious individual life in season through Abraham's invitation; you have arrived in the appointed place as ordered by the Commander of Revelation. You have changed the dress of your individual life into the white dress of death. You have stepped off of your carpet in *jihad* and on the carpet of God as a guest in the land of faith. You have pledged your allegiance to the Right Hand of God; have drowned 'self' in the whirlpool of love; have negated 'self' in the circumambulating masses; have arrived at your 'self', being cleansed of the dust of life and, little by little, of the rust of your 'self'; have arisen out of the whirlpool; have endeavored in the wondrous and thirsty mountains searching for water; then, have fallen, all at once from Makkah to Arafah;

you were already w/ him

from there, station by station, you have returned to God. You have collected weapons in consciousness under the brilliant sun of knowledge; have gathered arms in consciousness during the reign of darkness and the dissimulation of night; have passed the frontier of Mina in harmony with time and company of the congregation; have attached and in the first attack, have destroyed the last base. Then freed, you have released the land of faith and love from the sovereignity of Iblis. You have attained the station of Abraham, have ascended to the peak higher than martyrdom and, at the end, you have sacrificed a sheep.

Where do you go? What do you do? What have you attained at the termination of the greatest spiritual journey, having attained the place of the highest ascent of the human being, having passed through the most perilous places, displaying creation: monotheism (*tawhid*), self-sacrifice (*ithar*), jihad, martyrdom, battle against Iblis, victory over the station of love? What do you do?

Slaughter. Slaughter a sheep. Why? What is the philosophy behind this? What is the secret? What is the purpose of slaughtering a sheep? Finally, what is the hajj which speaks of total faith?

I dare not speak. It is unbelievable for us and our religious spirit. Let God Himself answer and reveal the reason why: "*So eat thereof and feed the abased poor.*" (22:28) Feed the silent, poor man and oppressed seeker of justice. And again, "*and feed the needy, the supplicant.*" (22:36) This means: fight poverty. At the end of the way, help a hungry person, help an oppressed person with some of what you eat. That is all!

THE RETURN

O haj! Where are you going now? Towards your home? The world? Are you leaving the hajj as you had come? Never!

O you who, in secret, played the role of Abraham in this scene!

A good actor or actress is dissolved in the personality whose role he or she is playing. If you have played your role well, the scene will end, but not your work. Some artists have never left the role they had in the scene and have died with it.

And you, O you who had to play the role of Abraham, not in jest but in worship, with love, do not leave the House of God and simply return to your own home; do not return from the role of Abraham to the role of self.

Do not leave the House of the People. Do not again restrict yourself. Do not leave the *ihram*; do not put on your own clothes.

Return from Mina to Makkah with your Ishmael.

You are Abraham, history's great idol-destroyer, the founder of monotheism in the world, who carried the mission to guide the people upon his shoulders, the 'patient-rebellious', the 'rebel-guide', a Prophet: anguish in his soul' love in his heart' enlightened mind and...an axe in his hand.

The manifestation of faith arising from out of the heart of infidelity (*kufr*); the geyser of monotheism (*tawhid*) arising from out of the swamp of multitheism (*shirk*).

Abraham—the idol-destroyer of mankind's tribe— from the home of Azar—the idol-carver of his tribe!

The idol-destroyer, Nimrod-destructor, crusher of ignorance and tyranny; the enemy of sleep; the rebel against the tranquility of humiliation and the security of oppression; the leader of a tribe; the pioneer of the Movement: life, motion, direction, idea, hope, faith and monotheism.

You are Abraham! Step into the midst of the fire— the fire of tyranny, ignorance—in order to save humanity from the fire—the fire of tyranny, ignorance.

The fire which is part of the destiny of each responsible human being, responsible for illumination and salvation.

But the God of monotheism turns the fire of Nimrodians into a red rose for the Abrahamians!

You will not be burned. You will not turn into ashes. The purpose was that you move through *jihad* by going towards...the fire so that the 'self' is offered in moving to save the masses from the fire,

Until the most painful of martyrdoms.

You are Abraham! Sacrifice your Ishmael with your own two hands. Place your knife at his throat.

In order to remove the knife from the throat of the masses, the masses who have continuously been slaughtered at the feet of palaces of power built from plundered treasures and at the threshold of deceiving, humiliating temples, place the blade against the throat of your own Ishmael so that you gain the power to take the blade away from the executioner.

But...the God of Abraham Himself pays the ransom for all Ishmaels.

You do not kill. You do not lose your Ishmael. The purpose is to move in the Way of Faith to the point where you have sacrificed your Ishmael with both hands. Until...more painful than martyrdom.

And now, O you who have come from the circumambulation of love, you are standing at the Station of Abraham; you have reached the Station of Abraham!

And when Abraham had reached here, he had passed the many phases of his eventful life from the breaking of idols, the destroying of Nimrod, the bearing of torture, the suffering of the fire, the struggling against Iblis, the sacrificing of Ishmael and...migrations, wanderings, lonelinesses, tortures and passing from prophethood to leadership. *"Behold I make you an Imam for the people."* (2:124)

From individuality to the congregation; from being the son of the house of Azar, the idol-carver to becoming the founder of the House of Monotheism!

And now, he stands here, the snow of age upon his head, at the end of a life which resembles a history, appointed to build the House, to install the Black Stone, the Hand of God in the House of God; and his partner—Ishmael—who carries stones and hands them to his father. While standing upon this stone, his father lays the foundation of the House and builds it!

O wonder! Ishmael and Abraham are building the Ka'bah; Ishmael and Abraham—one passed through the fire and the other, the altar of sacrifice. Now, both are agents of God, responsible for the masses, architects of the most ancient temple of monotheism upon the earth, the first House of the People in history, the House of the Free, liberty, the Ka'bah of love, worship, a sanctuary, a mystery among the mysteries of the tent of 'cover, chastity and the angelic world'.

And now you are standing in the Station of Abraham, stepping in the footprint of Abraham, upon the last step of the ladder of Abraham's descent, at the highest peak of Abraham's miraj, in the closest distance of Abraham to nearness.

The Station of Abraham!

And you, the founder of the Ka'bah, the architect of the House of Freedom, the founder of monotheism, responsible, lover, aware, idol-destroyer, leader of the tribes, opposed to Nimrod's oppression, in combat against the ignorance of multitheism, in *jihad* against the temptations of Iblis, the satan (*khanas*) who places temptation in the breasts of the people.

Bearing homelessness, anguish, danger, fire and the slaughter of your Ishmael; and now, no longer a House for your 'self' or a base for your Ishmael but a House for the People, a shelter for the shelterless, a place secure for those pursued, the fugitives, the injured, the hunted who, bloodied and in fear, wander the earth, frightened and wounded; who find no shelter as everywhere Nimrod is in pursuit.

A torch in this dark and longest night of the winter solstice.

A cry on this night of tyranny.

A sanctuary, secure, clear and free for humanity, for the Family of God—the people—because everywhere disgrace and insecurity rule. They have made the earth into a grand house of prostitution, a place of murder, where every deed is forbidden except aggression and discrimination. O you who appear in Abraham's role, who stand in Abraham's Station, who stand upon the footstep of Abraham and who give the hand of allegiance to the Hand of Abraham's God:

Live like Abraham and in your own age, be the architect of the Ka'bah of faith. Move your people out from the stagnant swamp of life, from the dead-like living, from the quite sleep of the abasement of tyranny and from the darkness of ignorance; give them direction; call them to the hajj; circumambulate.

And you, O ally of God! O in step with Abraham! O you who have come from the circumambulation, you who have ended your desire with the *tawaf al-nisa*, you who have come from the annihilation of 'self' in the circumambulating masses! You who have emerged in the shape of Abraham, who are standing in the place of the architect of the Ka'bah, founder of the sacred city, the Masjid al-Haram, and face to face with your ally—God!

Make your land a sacred area
For you are in the sacred area.
Make your age a sacred time
For you are in the sacred time.
Make the earth into a sacred mosque
For you are in the Masjid al-Haram.
For 'the earth is God's mosque'
And you see that:
It is not.

Moral imperative

...nariati shit'e muslim
  - Iranian revolution
    Red Shi'ite muslim

★ Every day is (Ashura) every land is karbula
(Karbala) → 680 - day
    Husayn becomes a martyr
      for shi'is - as so they
    must celebrate
        clear parallels to christ
        w/ redemptive suffering
_____

- constancy and change in form
     + meaning
- personal formation/transformation
- cultivation of sentiment and emotion
- marking and tranforming time +
   space
- commemoration of myth + history
- affirmation of group unity or distiction
- complex social patterns involving
   religious, political, and
   socio economic element s